Vocabulary
AND
Composition
Through
Pleasurable
Reading

BOOK I

AMSCO SCHOOL PUBLICATIONS, INC.,
a division of Perfection Learning®

Acknowledgments

Grateful acknowledgment is made to the following sources for having granted permission to reprint copyrighted materials.

Brandt & Brandt. *Selection 6.* From "The Most Dangerous Game" by Richard Connell. Copyright 1924 by Richard Connell. Copyright renewed © 1952, by Louise Fox Connell. Reprinted by permission of Brandt & Brandt Literary Agents, Inc.

Harcourt Brace Jovanovich, Inc. *Selection 9.* Excerpt from "A Nice Old-Fashioned Romance" in MY NAME IS ARAM, copyright 1940 and renewed 1968 by William Saroyan, reprinted by permission of Harcourt Brace Jovanovich, Inc.

Houghton Mifflin Company

Selection 3. From THE MEMBER OF THE WEDDING by Carson McCullers. Copyright 1946 by Carson McCullers. Copyright renewed © 1974 by Floria V. Lasky. Reprinted by permission of Houghton Mifflin Company.

Selection 8. From SHANE by Jack Schaefer. Copyright 1949 by Jack Schaefer. Copyright © renewed 1976 by Jack Schaefer. Reprinted by permission of Houghton Mifflin Company.

Selection 11. From JOHNNY TREMAIN by Esther Forbes. Copyright 1943 by Esther Forbes Hoskins. Copyright © renewed 1971 by Linwood M. Erskine, Jr., Executor of the Estate. Reprinted by permission of Houghton Mifflin Company.

Alfred A. Knopf, Inc. *Selection 2.* From THE LIGHT IN THE FOREST by Conrad Richter. Copyright 1953 by Curtis Publishing Company. Copyright 1953 by Conrad Richter. Reprinted by permission of Alfred A. Knopf, Inc.

Harold Ober Associates Inc. *Selection 12.* From THE LILIES OF THE FIELD by William E. Barrett. Copyright 1962 by William E. Barrett. Copyright renewed 1990 by William E. Barrett, Jr. Reprinted by permission of Harold Ober Associates Incorporated.

Penguin USA. *Selection 13.* From THE RED PONY by John Steinbeck. Copyright 1933, 1937, 1938 © renewed 1961, 1965, 1966 by John Steinbeck. Used by permission of Viking Penguin, a division of Penguin Books USA Inc.

G. P. Putnam's Sons. *Selection 5.* From FAMOUS NEGRO HEROES OF AMERICA by Langston Hughes. Copyright © 1958 by Langston Hughes. Used by permission of G. P. Putnam's Sons. Original publisher Dodd, Mead & Company.

© 2015 by Amsco School Publications, Inc.,
a division of Perfection Learning®

This edition is a major revision of *Vocabulary Through Pleasurable Reading, Book I,* © *1974 by Amsco School Publications, Inc.*

Please visit our websites at:
www.amscopub.com and *www.perfectionlearning.com*

When ordering this book, please specify:
ISBN 978-0-87720-769-6 or **13536**

Vocabulary
AND
Composition

Through
Pleasurable
Reading

BOOK I

HAROLD LEVINE

Chairman Emeritus of English,
Benjamin Cardozo High School, New York

NORMAN LEVINE

Associate Professor of English,
City College of the City University of New York

ROBERT T. LEVINE

Professor of English
North Carolina A & T State University

Vocabulary books by the authors

A Scholarship Vocabulary Program, Courses I–III
Vocabulary and Composition Through Pleasurable Reading, Books I–VI
Vocabulary for Enjoyment, Books I–III
Vocabulary for the High School Student, Books A, B
Vocabulary for the High School Student
Vocabulary for the College-Bound Student
The Joy of Vocabulary

To the Student

Where did famous writers learn their composition skills? To a large extent, from other famous writers—and you can do the same. You will learn many valuable writing skills from sixteen famous authors in the composition strand that runs through this book, alongside the reading and vocabulary strands.

Each unit in this book begins with an unusually interesting passage from a widely read work, such as *The Tell-Tale Heart*, *The Light in the Forest*, *The Member of the Wedding*, *The Call of the Wild*, *Gulliver's Travels*, and *The Red Pony*. This carefully chosen passage is the source and inspiration for everything you will learn in the unit, not only about writing, but also about critical thinking (reading) and, of course, vocabulary.

That, briefly, is the plan and purpose of this book. Now, try the unit beginning on page 1, or any of the other units, so that you may see for yourself how rewarding and enjoyable it can be to improve your VOCABULARY AND COMPOSITION THROUGH PLEASURABLE READING.

The Authors

For Your Reading Pleasure

UNIT III / Reading Selections 9–12

UNIT IV / Reading Selections 13–16

The Tell-Tale Heart

by Edgar Allan Poe

Read this opening selection of a short story that has sent chills down millions of spines.

True!—nervous—very, very dreadfully nervous I had been and am! but why *will* you say that I am mad? The disease had sharpened my senses—not destroyed—not dulled them. Above all was the sense of hearing acute. I heard all things in the heaven and in the

5   earth. I heard many things in hell. How, then, am I mad? Hearken! and observe how healthily—how calmly I can tell you the whole story.

It is impossible to say how first the idea entered my brain: but once conceived, it haunted me day and night. Object there was

10 none. Passion there was none. I loved the old man. He had never wronged me. He had never given me insult. For his gold I had no desire. I think it was his eye! yes, it was this! One of his eyes resembled that of a vulture—a pale blue eye, with a film over it. Whenever it fell upon me, my blood ran cold; and so by degrees—

15 very gradually—I made up my mind to take the life of the old man, and thus rid myself of the eye for ever.

Now this is the point. You fancy me mad. Madmen know nothing. But you should have seen *me*. You should have seen how wisely I proceeded—with what caution—with what foresight—with

20 what dissimulation I went to work!

I was never kinder to the old man than during the whole week before I killed him. And every night, about midnight, I turned the latch of his door and opened it—oh, so gently! And then, when I had made an opening sufficient for my head, I put in a dark lan-

25 tern, all closed, closed, so that no light shone out, and then I thrust

in my head. Oh, you would have laughed to see how cunningly I thrust it in! I moved it slowly—very, very slowly, so that I might not disturb the old man's sleep. It took me an hour to place my whole head within the opening so far that I could see him as he

30 lay upon his bed. Ha!—would a madman have been so wise as this? And then, when my head was well in the room, I undid the lantern cautiously—oh, so cautiously—cautiously (for the hinges creaked)—I undid it just so much that a single thin ray fell upon the vulture eye. And this I did for seven long nights—every night just at mid-

35 night—but I found the eye always closed; and so it was impossible to do the work; for it was not the old man who vexed me, but his Evil Eye. And every morning, when the day broke, I went boldly into the chamber, and spoke courageously to him, calling him by name in a hearty tone, and inquiring how he had passed the night.

40 So you see he would have been a very profound old man, indeed, to suspect that every night, just at twelve, I looked in upon him while he slept.

Line 20: *dissimulation:* cunning

UNDERSTANDING THE SELECTION

Exercise 1.1: Close Reading

In the blank space, write the *letter* of the choice that best completes the statement or answers the question.

1. The narrator (the one who tells the story) is _____.

   (A) dreadfully nervous but not mad
   (B) mad
   (C) not too talkative

2. The narrator says that he has a very fine sense of _____.

   (A) hearing
   (B) sight
   (C) smell

3. The old man, according to the narrator, _____.

   (A) is a poor sleeper
   (B) has some money
   (C) has insulted the narrator

4. On each of his seven attempts to kill the old man, the narrator finds _____.

   (A) the door locked
   (B) the old man awake
   (C) the eye closed

5. The narrator _____.

   (A) wishes the old man were alive again
   (B) is not capable of constructing and carrying out a detailed plan
   (C) wants us to believe that he is perfectly sane

6. Which of the following is a TRUE statement? _____

   (A) The narrator is horrified by the thought of committing a murder.
   (B) The idea of killing the old man comes to the narrator rather suddenly.
   (C) The narrator does not claim to be perfect.

7. On every visit to the sleeping old man, the narrator _____.

   (A) arrives at a different time
   (B) allows some light to escape from the lantern
   (C) makes some noise

8. In the last paragraph of the reading selection, there is NO synonym for _____.

   (A) "room" (line 31)
   (B) "lantern" (lines 24–25)
   (C) "midnight" (line 22)

Going Over the Answers   How can you arrive at the right answers to reading questions like those you have just answered? There is one rule: *Never guess!* The proof for each right answer is in the passage. Find it. Here's how:

Question 1:   The narrator says he is "very, very dreadfully nervous," but as he continues to talk we realize that his condition is more serious. When he says, "I heard all things in the heaven and in the earth . . . I heard many things in hell," we know we are dealing with a madman. We are even more certain he is mad when he tells of his weird reason for wanting to kill the old man. We cannot say the narrator is "not too talkative" because he tells us everything. The answer, then, is (B) *mad*.

Question 2:   The narrator says, "Above all was the sense of hearing acute." This proves that the answer is (A) *hearing*.

Question 3:   The comment "For his gold I had no desire" suggests that the old man is not penniless. From what the narrator tells us, we know that the old man sleeps well and that he has not insulted the narrator. The answer, therefore, is (B) *has some money*.

Question 4:   The statement "but I found the eye always closed" proves that the answer is (C) *the eye closed*.

Question 5:   Such remarks as "How, then, am I mad?" and "would a madman have been so wise as this?" prove that the answer is (C) *wants us to believe that he is perfectly sane*. The narrator's strong desire to rid himself of the old man's eye forever shows that answer (A) cannot be right. His detailed plan for the murder, plus the manner in which he proceeds to carry it out, proves that answer (B) is incorrect, too.

Question 6: The narrator's admission in line 1—"True!—nervous—very, very dreadfully nervous I had been and am!"—shows that he does not claim to be perfect. The answer is (C).

Question 7: Lines 33–35 indicate that the narrator allows some light to fall on the "vulture eye" at midnight for seven nights in a row. The answer is therefore (B).

Question 8: "Chamber" (line 38) is a synonym for "room." "Twelve" (line 41) is a synonym for "midnight." However, there is no synonym for "lantern." The answer is (B).

LEARNING NEW WORDS

Line	Word	Meaning	Typical Use
4	**acute** *(adj.)* ə-'kyüt	1. keen; penetrating; sharp	Bloodhounds have a remarkably *acute* sense of smell.
		(ant. **dull, blunt***)*	Fortunately, the pain was *dull.*
			It is hard to cut meat with a *blunt* knife.
		2. serious and demanding attention; urgent; critical	Many new homes must be built to ease the *acute* housing shortage.
9	**conceive** *(v.)* kən-'sēv	take into the mind; think up; imagine	Stephenson *conceived* the idea for the steam engine by watching a boiling kettle.
15	**gradually** *(adv.)* 'graj-ə-wə-lē	little by little; by degrees	When a tire develops a slow leak, the air escapes so *gradually* that you won't even notice it at first.
39	**inquire** *(v.)* in-'kwīər	ask; seek information about	When I was ill, my friend called every day to *inquire* about my health.
9	**object** *(n.)* äb'-jikt	thing aimed at; purpose; aim	My *object* in calling you is to wish you a happy birthday.
6	**observe** *(v.)* əb-'zərv	perceive by paying careful attention; see; notice; watch	By *observing* my woodworking teacher, I learned how to use a saw correctly.

10	**passion** *(n.)* 'pash-ən	strong, overpowering feeling, such as love, hate, fear, anger, rage, etc.	The woman spoke of her neighbors with such *passion* that anyone could see how much she hated them.
40	**profound** *(adj.)* prə-'faünd	1. possessing insight (the power of seeing into a situation); discerning	This is an easy problem; you do not have to be very *profound* to solve it.
		(*ant.* **shallow**)	Their weak answers show that they have a *shallow* knowledge of the subject.
		2. very deep; deep-seated	The daring rescue aroused our *profound* admiration.
36	**vex** *(v.)* 'veks	bring trouble to; annoy	If our whispering *vexes* you, go to a quieter part of the library.
		(*ant.* **please**)	You will not *please* Mom if you try to help with what she is doing; you will only vex her.
13	**vulture** *(n.)* 'vəl-chər	large, hawk-like bird of prey that feeds on dead animals	*Vultures* quickly found the carcass of the deer abandoned by the hunters.

APPLYING WHAT YOU HAVE LEARNED

Exercise 1.2: Sentence Completion

Which of the two choices correctly completes the sentence? Write the *letter* of your answer in the space provided.

1. I can see by your _____ that you are vexed.

    A. relaxed manner   B. nail-biting

2. Don't _____; the situation is acute.

    A. delay   B. rush

3. Inquire at the _____.

    A. fire exit   B. information desk

4. Anyone who can explain how a nuclear reaction works cannot be too _____.

    A. profound   B. shallow

5. Many people I know seem to have no object in life. They ____.

    A. don't know where they are going   B. never interfere

6. The change occurred so gradually that I ____ it at the very beginning.

    A. noticed   B. did not notice

7. Mere ____ is not a passion.

    A. liking   B. anger

8. Whoever conceived this must have had ____.

    A. remarkable eyesight   B. a fine imagination

9. Observe what I am doing; do not ____.

    A. look the other way   B. watch everything I do

10. By their feeding habits, vultures ____ pollution in our forests.

    A. contribute to   B. help prevent

Exercise 1.3: Definitions

Each expression below defines a word taught on pages 4–5. Enter that word in the space provided.

_____ **1.** by degrees

_____ **2.** perceive by paying careful attention

_____ **3.** strong, overpowering feeling

_____ **4.** take into the mind

_____ **5.** thing aimed at

_____ **6.** bird of prey

_____ **7.** seek information about

_____ **8.** serious and demanding attention

_____ **9.** very deep

_____ **10.** bring trouble to

UNDERSTANDING SYNONYMS AND ANTONYMS

    A **synonym** is a word _similar_ in meaning to another word. _Autumn_ and _fall_ are synonyms.

    An **antonym** is a word _opposite_ in meaning to another word. _Beginning_ and _ending_ are antonyms.

Exercise 1.4: Synonyms and Antonyms

Fill the blanks in column A with the required synonyms or antonyms, selecting them from column B.

	Column A	Column B
_____	1. synonym for *perceive*	annoyance
_____	2. antonym for *sharp*	observe
_____	3. antonym for *please*	vex
_____	4. synonym for *think up*	blunt
_____	5. synonym for *vexation*	shallow
_____	6. synonym for *aim*	conceivable
_____	7. antonym for *profound*	conceive
_____	8. synonym for *imaginable*	acute
_____	9. antonym for *dull*	vexing
_____	10. synonym for *annoying*	object

LEARNING SOME ROOTS AND DERIVATIVES

Suppose you have just learned that the noun *passion* means "strong feeling." Now, if you were to meet the adjective *passionate* (he made a *passionate* protest), you could easily tell that it means "full of passion or strong feeling." Also, if you were to come across the adverb *passionately* (he protested *passionately*), you would know that it means "with passion or strong feeling," or "in a passionate manner."

A word like *passionate* or *passionately* is called a **derivative** because it is derived (formed) from another word.

A word like *passion* from which other words are derived is called a **root**.

Each word in boldfaced type is a *root*. The words below it are its *derivatives*.

acute *(adj.)*	I had an *acute* interest in your problem.
acutely *(adv.)*	I was *acutely* interested in your problem.
conceive *(v.)*	We could *conceive* of no way to escape.
conceivable *(adj.)*	There was no *conceivable* way for us to escape.
inconceivable *(adj.)*	Escape was *inconceivable*.

gradual (adj.)	The change was *gradual*.
gradually (adv.)	The change came about *gradually*.
inquire (v.)	Let me be the one to *inquire*.
inquirer (n.)	Let me be the *inquirer*.
inquiry (n.)	Let me make the *inquiry*.
observe (v.)	From here, you can easily *observe* the stage.
observable (adj.)	From here, the stage is easily *observable*.
observation (n.)	From here, *observation* of the stage will be easy.
observer (n.)	From here, an *observer* can easily get a good view of the stage.
passion (n.)	The losers protested with *passion*.
passionate (adj.)	The losers made a *passionate* protest.
passionately (adv.)	The losers protested *passionately*.
profound (adj.)	I have a *profound* respect for inventors.
profoundly (adv.)	I respect inventors *profoundly*.
vex (v.)	Don't let the delay *vex* you.
vexation (n.)	Don't let the delay cause you any *vexation*.

Exercise 1.5: Roots and Derivatives

Fill each blank below with the root or derivative just listed that best completes the sentence.

1. If you will make your _____ more clear, I shall try to answer it.

2. Doreen's talk about quitting school caused her parents a great deal of _____ .

3. As dawn approaches, the stars become less and less _____ .

4. Lassie's sense of smell is keener than ours. Also, she hears more _____ .

5. Improvement does not take place all at once; it is a(n) _____

   process.

6. A careful _____ would have noticed immediately that something

   was wrong.

7. The incident made no deep impression on Ben, but it influenced me _____ .

8. I never imagined that Terry would move. Such an idea was not _____ .

9. Steve did not ask the question. I was the _____ .

10. When we are overcome by strong emotion, we speak _____ .

A *suffix* is a sound added to the end of a word to form a new word:

WORD	SUFFIX	NEW WORD
profound	+ -ly (in a ____ manner)	= profound*ly* (in a profound manner)

Study these suffixes and their meanings:

SUFFIX	MEANING	SAMPLE WORD
-able	able to be	observ*able* (able to be observed)
-ation	act of	observ*ation* (act of observing)
-er	one who	observ*er* (one who observes)
-ly	in a ____ manner	courageous*ly* (in a courageous manner)
-ed	ending of past participle	Yesterday I observ*ed* them.
-ing	ending of present participle	Today I am observ*ing* them.

You always have to know whether the suffix you are attaching begins with a *vowel* or a *consonant*. Therefore, review the following:

The *vowels* are the letters **a**, **e**, **i**, **o**, and **u**.
All the other letters are *consonants*.

Question: What happens to the **e** at the end of a word when we add a suffix?

Answers: (1) If the suffix begins with a *vowel*, drop the **e**.

observe̸ + able = observable

We drop the **e** because the suffix **able** begins with **a**, a *vowel*.

(2) If the suffix begins with a *consonant*, keep the **e**.

acute + ly = acutely

We keep the **e** because the suffix **ly** begins with **l**, a *consonant*.

Study these further examples. Then do the exercise that follows.

observe̸ + ation = observation
conceive̸ + ed = conceived
conceive̸ + ing = conceiving
observe̸ + er = observer
But:
gradual + ly = gradually

Exercise 1.6: Wordbuilding With Suffixes

Complete the following:

1. profound + ly = _____
2. conceive + ed = _____
3. vex + ation = _____
4. observe + er = _____
5. vex + ing = _____
6. blunt + ly = _____
7. inquire + ing = _____
8. observe + able = _____
9. passionate + ly = _____
10. acute + ly = _____
11. imagine + ation = _____
12. conceive + ing = _____
13. keen + ly = _____
14. imagine + able = _____
15. inquire + er = _____
16. critical + ly = _____
17. observe + ed = _____
18. discerning + ly = _____
19. trouble + ing = _____
20. conceive + able = _____

Exercise 1.7: Conciseness

State each expression below *concisely* (as briefly as possible). Hint: Enter a single word ending in one of the suffixes taught on page 9.

1. act of imagining: _____
2. one who inquires: _____
3. in a passionate manner: _____
4. able to be conceived: _____
5. one who observes: _____
6. in a profound manner: _____
7. act of vexing: _____
8. present participle of conceive: _____
9. act of observing: _____
10. past participle of perceive: _____

To use your dictionary intelligently, you must know the meaning of abbreviations like **n.**, **adj.**, **v.**, and **adv.**

A **noun** *(n.)* is a word that names a person, place, thing, or condition. In the following passage, all the boldfaced words are nouns:

The **narrator** in this strange **tale** very obviously suffers from a serious mental **illness**. His **plot** against a completely innocent old **man** is a clear **sign** of **insanity**.

An **adjective** *(adj.)* is a word that modifies (describes) a noun. The following words in the passage above are adjectives:

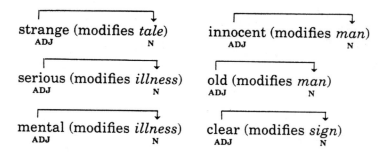

strange (modifies *tale*) innocent (modifies *man*)

serious (modifies *illness*) old (modifies *man*)

mental (modifies *illness*) clear (modifies *sign*)

A **verb** *(v.)* is a word that expresses action or a state of being. The verbs in the passage above are *suffers* and *is*.

An **adverb** *(adv.)* is a word that modifies a verb, an adjective, or another adverb. These are the adverbs in the passage above:

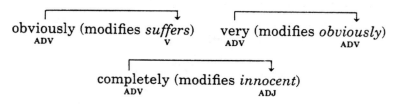

obviously (modifies *suffers*) very (modifies *obviously*)

completely (modifies *innocent*)

Let us look at the passage once more to sum up the parts of speech we have so far discussed.

The narrator in this strange tale very obviously
suffers from a serious mental illness. His plot against a
completely innocent old man is a clear sign of insanity.

Exercise 1.8: Changing One Part of Speech to Another

Sample: Change the adjective *passionate* to an adverb.

Answer: **passionately**

Sample: From what verb is the noun *observation* derived?

Answer: **observe**

1. From what verb is the noun *inquiry* derived? _____
2. Change the adjective *profound* to an adverb. _____
3. Change the adverb *gradually* to an adjective. _____
4. Change the verb *vex* to a noun. _____
5. Write an adjective ending in *-able* that we get from the verb *conceive.* _____
6. Change the adverb *acutely* to an adjective. _____
7. Write a noun ending in *-er* that we get from the verb *observe.* _____
8. Write a noun ending in *-er* that we get from the verb *inquire.* _____
9. Change the adverb *passionately* to a noun. _____
10. Write an adjective ending in *-able* that we get from the verb *observe.* _____

IMPROVING YOUR COMPOSITION SKILLS: REDUCING OR AVOIDING REPETITION

Edgar Allan Poe uses "midnight" in lines 22 and 34–35, but when he has to express the same idea in line 41, he avoids "midnight" because it would have been too repetitious—perhaps even boring. Instead, he uses a synonym—"twelve."

Likewise, in line 38, he does not repeat "room," which he has used in line 31, but he conveys the same idea through the synonym "chamber."

Exercise 1.9: Reducing Repetition

Replace the boldfaced repeated word with a suitable synonym. The first replacement has been entered as a sample.

1. Were you able to see well? I thought it would be hard to see from the seat I had, but

   I was able to **see** everything. ___**observe**___

2. The President was eager for the questioning to end, but the reporters continued to ask questions. Finally, he said that he would allow only one more **question.** _____

3. She claimed her purpose in coming was to learn about our club. Was that her true purpose, or did she have some other **purpose** in mind? _____

4. He still has keen vision and a keen mind, but his hearing is not so **keen** as it used to be. _____

5. What a fine imagination you have! No one else could have imagined a more brilliant idea than yours. I could never have **imagined** it. _____

Exercise 1.10: Avoiding Repetition

Read the following paragraph and answer the questions. The first one has been answered as a sample.

> Then something inconceivable happened—the umpire reversed his decision. You can easily conceive how this enraged the fans—they just could not stop booing. Though their rage was slow to cool, they eventually quieted down,
> 5 the stadium slowly returned to normal, and we went on to lose the game. Obviously, the upsetting decision made a deep impression on many of the fans and players. They were deeply troubled by it, and it is still troubling some of them.

Question 1. The word **conceive** (line 2) repeats a part of **inconceivable** (line 1). What word can replace **conceive?**

Answer: ___imagine___

Question 2. What can replace **rage** (line 4), which is too much like **enraged** (line 3)?

Answer: _____

Question 3. What can replace **slowly** (line 5), which is too much like **slow** (line 4)?

Answer: _____

Question 4. What can replace **deeply** (line 8), which is too much like **deep** (line 7)?

Answer: _____

Question 5. What can replace **troubling** (line 8), which is too much like **troubled** (line 8)?

Answer: _____

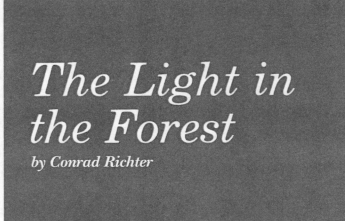

The Light in the Forest

by Conrad Richter

Suppose you had been adopted by an Indian tribe as a very young child, and now, several years later, the Indians are being compelled to return you to your people. How would you feel about leaving?

The boy was about fifteen years old. He tried to stand very straight and still when he heard the news, but inside of him everything had gone black. It wasn't that he couldn't endure pain. In summer he would put a stone hot from the fire on his flesh to see

5 how long he could stand it. In winter he would sit in the icy river until his Indian father smoking on the bank said he could come out. It made him strong against any hardship that would come to him, his father said. But if it had any effect on this thing that had come to him now, the boy couldn't tell what it was.

10 For days word had been reaching the Indian village that the Lenni Lenape and Shawanose must give up their white prisoners. Never for a moment did the boy dream that it meant him. Why, he had been one of them ever since he could remember! Cuyloga was his father. Eleven years past he had been adopted to take the

15 place of a son dead from the yellow vomit. More than once he had been told how, when he was only four years old, his father had said words that took out his white blood and put Indian blood in its place. His white thoughts and meanness had been wiped away and the brave thoughts of the Indian put in their stead. Ever since,

20 he had been True Son, the blood of Cuyloga and flesh of his flesh. For eleven years he had lived here, a native of this village on the Tuscarawas, a full member of the family. Then how could he be torn from his home like a sapling from the ground and given to the alien whites who were his enemy!

14

25   The day his father told him, the boy made up his mind. Never would he give up his Indian life. Never! When no one saw him, he crept away from the village. From an old campfire, he blackened his face. Up above Pockhapockink, which means the stream between two hills, he had once found a hollow tree. Now he hid

30 himself in it. He thought only he knew the existence of that tree and was dismayed when his father tracked him to it. It was humiliating to be taken back with his blackened face and tied up in his father's cabin like some prisoner to be burned at the stake. When his father led him out next morning, he knew everybody watched:

35 his mother and sisters, the townspeople, his uncle and aunt, his cousins and his favorite cousin, Half Arrow, with whom he had ever fished, hunted, and played. Seldom had they been separated even for a single day.

     All morning on the path with his father, crazy thoughts ran

40 like squirrels in the boy's head. Never before had he known his father to be in the wrong. Could it be that he was in the right now? Had he unknowingly left a little white blood in the boy's veins and was it for this that he must be returned? Then they came in sight of the ugly log redoubts and pale tents of the white

45 army, and the boy felt sure there was in his body not a drop of blood that knew these things. At the sight and smells of the white man, strong aversion and loathing came over him. He tried with all his young strength to get away. His father had to hold him hard. In the end he dragged him twisting and yelling over the

50 ground to the council house of the whites and threw him on the leaves that had been spread around.

     "I gave talking paper that I bring him," he told the white guards. "Now he belong to you."

     It was all over then, the boy knew. He was as good as dead and

55 lay among the other captives with his face down. He was sure that his father had stayed. He could feel his presence and smell the sweet inner bark of the red willow mixed with the dried sumach leaves of his pipe. When dusk fell, a white guard came up. The other soldiers called him Del, perhaps because he could talk Del-

60 aware, the strange name the whites gave the Lenni Lenape and their language. True Son heard Del tell his father that all Indians must be out of the camp by nightfall. From the sounds the boy guessed his father was knocking out his pipe and putting it away. Then he knew he had risen and was standing over him.

65   "Now go like an Indian, True Son," he said in a low, stern voice. "Give me no more shame."

Line 44. *redoubts:* forts

Exercise 2.1: Close Reading

In the blank space, write the *letter* of the choice that best completes the statement.

1. Cuyloga adopted True Son to replace a son who had _____ .

    (A) died in battle
    (B) been taken prisoner by the whites
    (C) died of disease

2. True Son _____ .

    (A) hates his Indian father
    (B) has no memory at all of his white father
    (C) is not fully accepted by his Indian family

3. The selection suggests that, when he loses True Son, Cuyloga will be left _____ .

    (A) without a son
    (B) with one son
    (C) without any children

4. Cuyloga considers it a disgrace that _____ .

    (A) he should have to hand over True Son
    (B) True Son should show that he does not obey him
    (C) True Son should have played with Half Arrow

5. True Son has been away from the white people for _____ years.

    (A) four
    (B) fifteen
    (C) eleven

6. There is reason to believe that _____ .

    (A) Del has Indian blood in his veins
    (B) the Lenni Lenape are not free to do as they wish
    (C) True Son has never been told that he was adopted

7. Delaware, as used in the passage, is the name of a _____ .

    (A) river and a people
    (B) place
    (C) people and a language

8. After being turned over to the whites, True Son has to rely on his senses of _____ to obtain information about Cuyloga.

    (A) smell and hearing   (B) sight, smell, and hearing   (C) sight and smell

Line	Word	Meaning	Typical Use
47	**aversion** (n.) ə-'vər-zhən	distaste for something coupled with a desire to avoid it; dislike; antipathy (*ant.* **liking, fondness**)	Some people have an *aversion* to cats; others are fond of them.
55	**captive** (n.) 'kap-tiv	one that is taken and held prisoner	The treaty of peace requires both sides to release all *captives* immediately.
50	**council** (adj.) 'kaȯn-səl	used for a *council* (meeting or conference)	The meeting began as soon as the committee members had taken their seats around the *council* table.
	council (n.) 'kaȯn-səl	group of advisers	The President summoned his *council* to an emergency meeting.
31	**dismay** (v.) dis-'mā	cause to lose courage through alarm or fear; alarm; trouble greatly; horrify	We are *dismayed* by the vast problems before us, but we shall not give up.
58	**dusk** (n.) 'dəsk	time just before dark; darkness or partial darkness	With *dusk* approaching, it became more and more difficult to see the road ahead.
29	**hollow** (adj.) 'häl-ō	having nothing inside; empty; not solid (*ant.* **filled, solid**)	A handle that feels too light may be *hollow* inside.
31–2	**humiliate** (v.) hyü-'mil-ē-ˌāt	lower one's pride, dignity, or self-respect; mortify	Your father *humiliated* Louise when he scolded her in the presence of her friends.
47	**loathing** (n.) 'lō-t͟hiŋ	strong disgust; intense aversion (*ant.* **love**)	During my illness I had a *loathing* for food and ate very little.
23	**sapling** (n.) 'sap-liŋ	young tree	Deer love to chew the tender bark of *saplings*.

| 37 | **seldom** *(adv.)* | not often; infrequently; | You can usually count on Gail's |
| | 'sel-dəm | rarely | being at the meeting; she is *sel-dom* absent. |

*(ant. **often**)*

APPLYING WHAT YOU HAVE LEARNED

Exercise 2.2:   Sentence Completion

Which of the two choices correctly completes the sentence? Write the *letter* of your answer in the space provided.

1. In most homes, a _____ is seldom used.

(A) fire extinguisher   (B) can opener

2. Lights are usually turned _____ at dusk.

(A) on   (B) off

3. The announcement of election results can be humiliating for a _____ candidate.

(A) victorious   (B) defeated

4. There was _____ to eat in that walnut; it was hollow.

(A) nothing   (B) plenty

5. Anyone with a loathing for young children _____ be a baby-sitter.

(A) should   (B) should not

6. A _____ is nothing to be dismayed at.

(A) lost glove   (B) fractured leg

7. The pine sapling _____ .

(A) towered above our heads   (B) was about knee-high

8. Then we came to the council ground where the Indians used to _____ .

(A) meet   (B) hunt

9. Many students have an aversion for _____ .

(A) tests   (B) vacations

10. A captive _____ .

(A) makes frequent arrests   (B) is kept under guard

Exercise 2.3: Definitions

Each expression below defines a word taught on pages 17–18. Enter that word in the space provided.

_____ **1.** not often

_____ **2.** having nothing inside

_____ **3.** one that is taken and held prisoner

_____ **4.** strong disgust

_____ **5.** time just before dark

_____ **6.** distaste for something coupled with a desire to avoid it

_____ **7.** lower one's pride

_____ **8.** group of advisers

_____ **9.** young tree

_____ **10.** cause to lose courage through alarm

Exercise 2.4: Synonyms and Antonyms

A. Replace the italicized word with a *synonym* from the vocabulary list below.

_____ **1.** Who brought in the *captive?*

_____ **2.** They disappeared in the deepening *dusk.*

_____ **3.** Your thoughtless remark *mortified* my friend.

_____ **4.** The clubhouse will have several *meeting* rooms.

_____ **5.** We were *dismayed* to learn of the fatal accident.

B. Replace the italicized word with an *antonym* from the vocabulary list below.

_____ **6.** A *solid* wall separated the two rooms.

_____ **7.** When I was younger, I *loathed* fudge.

_____ **8.** They complained *infrequently.*

_____ **9.** Her mild interest in the subject developed into a passionate *fondness.*

_____ **10.** The bird's *captivity* did not last very long.

Vocabulary List

hollow	aversion	often
humiliated	prisoner	horrified
freedom	loved	seldom
council	filled	darkness

HOMONYMS

A **homonym** is a word that has the same pronunciation as another word but a different meaning. Here are some sets of homonyms:

ate (my lunch)   *hear* (listen)
eight (o'clock)   *here* (in this place)

pair (two)   *tail* (of an animal)
pear (fruit)   *tale* (story)

Two more homonyms are *council* and *counsel*.
We already know that the noun *council* means a meeting or conference.
This is a good time to learn that the noun *counsel* means (1) advice, or (2) a person who gives advice about the law; a lawyer.

Exercise 2.5: *Council* or *Counsel*?

1. The Governor has invited several distinguished citizens to a _____ on education.
2. If you have no _____, the court will appoint a lawyer to defend you.
3. Our class president attended a _____ on community problems.
4. In this matter I am depending on your _____.
5. The witness refused to answer the question on the advice of _____.

LEARNING SOME ROOTS AND DERIVATIVES

Each word in bold type is a **root**. The words below it are its **derivatives**.

averse *(adj.)*	I am *averse* to getting up early on a holiday.
aversion *(n.)*	I have an *aversion* to getting up early on a holiday.
captive *(adj.)*	The *captive* tourists were questioned for four hours.
captive *(n.)*	They were *captives* for four hours.
captivity *(n.)*	They were held in *captivity* for four hours.
council *(n.)*	Where will the *council* be held?
council *(adj.)*	We usually meet in the *council* room.

dismay *(v.)*	These unexpected problems *dismay* us.
dismay *(n.)*	They fill us with *dismay*.
dismaying *(adj.)*	They are *dismaying*.
dusk *(n.)*	*Dusk* was falling.
dusky *(adj.)*	It was becoming *dusky*.
hollow *(adj.)*	The wall is not solid; it has a *hollow* ring.
hollow *(n.)*	He scooped up some water in the *hollow* of his hand.
humiliate *(v.)*	The 9–0 loss *humiliated* us.
humiliating *(adj.)*	It was a *humiliating* defeat.
humiliatingly *(adv.)*	We were *humiliatingly* beaten.
humiliation *(n.)*	Have you ever suffered the *humiliation* of defeat?
loathe *(v.)*	There is no good reason why children should *loathe* vegetables?
loathsome *(adj.)*	Why do they find vegetables *loathsome*?
loathing *(n.)*	Why do they have a *loathing* for vegetables?

Exercise 2.6: Roots and Derivatives

Fill each blank below with the root or derivative just listed that best completes the sentence.

1. Someone shouted "Fire!" The lights went out. We rushed for the exit in terror and _____ .

2. The conference room has a large _____ table.

3. The proud honor student considered any mark below 90 as _____ low.

4. I used to _____ chopped spinach, but now I like it.

5. Only once during their _____ were the war prisoners allowed to write to their families.

6. A small animal can easily hide in the _____ of a tree.

7. After the sun had set, it became too _____ to read outdoors.

8. Everyone else is in favor of my plan. Why are you so _____ to it?

9. If you criticize your sister in the presence of her friends, she will lose face. Surely you don't want to _____ her!

10. Your strong disgust at the sight of a bug, worm, or ant shows that you think they are _____ .

IMPROVING YOUR SPELLING: ATTACHING -*ED* AND -*ING* TO WORDS ENDING IN -Y

ATTACHING -ED

Change *y* to *i* only if the letter before *y* is a consonant. Examples:

1. horrif$\overset{i}{y}$ + ed = horrified

QUESTION: Why was the *y* in **horrify** changed to *i*?
ANSWER: The letter before *y* is *f*, a *consonant*.

2. dismay + ed = dismayed

QUESTION: Why was the *y* in **dismay** not changed?
ANSWER: The letter before *y* is *a*, a *vowel*.

Memorize these exceptions: **laid, paid, said,** and their compounds (**mislaid, overpaid, unsaid,** etc.).

ATTACHING -ING

Do not change the *y* when adding -*ing*. Examples:

3. horrify + ing = horrifying
4. dismay + ing = dismaying

Exercise 2.7: Wordbuilding With -*ED* and -*ING*

Complete the following:

1. stay + ed =   _____
2. reply + ed =   _____
3. mortify + ing =   _____
4. mortify + ed =   _____
5. say + ed =   _____
6. cry + ing =   _____
7. cry + ed =   _____
8. repay + ed =   _____
9. fly + ing =   _____
10. bury + ed =   _____
11. annoy + ing =   _____
12. annoy + ed =   _____

13. lay + ing = _____

14. lay + ed = _____

15. display + ed = _____

16. reply + ing = _____

17. say + ing = _____

18. destroy + ed = _____

19. overpay + ed = _____

20. try + ed = _____

USES THAT A WORD MAY HAVE

The same word may be used as one part of speech in one sentence and another part of speech in another sentence. Look at these sentences:

1. We *love* freedom deeply.   (*love* is a verb)

2. We have a deep *love* of freedom.   (*love* is a noun)

Observe these three sentences:

3. Come to the *meeting*.   (*meeting* is a noun)

4. You know the *meeting* place.   (*meeting* is an adjective)

5. We are *meeting* resistance.   (*meeting* is a verb)

Important: To decide what part of speech a word is, see how it is used in its sentence.

Exercise 2.8: Adjective, Noun, or Verb
What part of speech is the italicized word?

1. Did you attend the *conference?*   _____

2. Where is the *conference* room?   _____

3. This defeat will not *dismay* us.   _____

4. There is no reason for *dismay*.   _____

5. Now go like an *Indian*.   _____

6. Never would he give up his *Indian* life.   _____

7. Few sights are as beautiful as *autumn* leaves.   _____

8. In *autumn* the leaves are beautiful.   _____

9. The *captive* was released unharmed.   _____

10. We couldn't leave. We were a *captive* audience.   _____

Exercise 2.9: Describing a Humiliating Experience

Reread lines 25–38 on page 15, in which True Son describes a humiliating experience. Then write a brief paragraph about a similar experience that you—or someone you know—had. If you cannot think of one, the following may give you an idea of what to write about.

1. Approaching your table with your lunch, you drop your tray.

2. You miss an easy question in class.

3. You make an error that causes your team to lose.

4. All your friends are going to a party to which you have not been invited.

5. You are defeated in a class election.

6. As you are about to pay for something, you find you do not have enough money.

Study this model answer based on suggestion 6, above.

MODEL PARAGRAPH ABOUT A HUMILIATING EXPERIENCE

Yesterday, as I was about to pay for my lunch in a downtown restaurant, I was dismayed to find that I did not have enough money. I was asked to wait for the manager. When he appeared, I said that I would go home and
5 return immediately with the rest of the money. However, he calmed me down and suggested I could bring it the next time I was in the neighborhood. I thanked him very much and left, feeling humiliated.

Hints From the Model Paragraph

The opening sentence (lines 1–3) tells not only WHAT happened (did not have enough money to pay for lunch) but also WHEN it happened (yesterday) and WHERE it happened (downtown restaurant). Try to do the same in your first sentence.

The rest of the paragraph gives additional details of the incident IN THE ORDER IN WHICH THEY HAPPENED. Try to use the same order when you give your details.

In a paragraph of this kind it is important to describe feelings. Note **dismayed** in the opening sentence and **humiliated** in the last sentence. Try to use these two key words in your own paragraph.

Now write your paragraph in the space below.

_____

_____

_____

_____

_____

_____

_____

_____

_____

_____

The Member of the Wedding

by Carson McCullers

Frankie, a motherless twelve-year-old girl, behaves strangely when she learns that her brother is about to get married and move away. She begins to call herself F. Jasmine, which she considers a more grown-up name, and she thinks that she, too, will leave town. First, though, she must say good-bye to the monkey and the monkey-man.

As F. Jasmine hurried down the street, she saw the two of them in her mind's eye—and wondered if they would remember her. The old Frankie had always loved the monkey and the monkey-man. They resembled each other—they both had an anxious, ques-
5 tioning expression, as though they wondered every minute if what they did was wrong. The monkey, in fact, was nearly always wrong; after he danced to the organ tune, he was supposed to take off his darling little cap and pass it around to the audience, but likely as not he would get mixed up and bow and reach out his cap
10 to the monkey-man, and not the audience. And the monkey-man would plead with him, and finally begin to chatter and fuss. When he would make as if to slap the monkey, the monkey would cringe down and chatter also—and they would look at each other with the same scared exasperation, their wrinkled faces very sad. After
15 watching them a long time, the old Frankie, fascinated, began to take on the same expression as she followed them around. And now F. Jasmine was eager to see them.

She could hear the broken-sounding organ plainly, although they were not on the main street, but up farther and probably just around the corner of the next block. So F. Jasmine hurried toward them. As she neared the corner, she heard other sounds that puzzled her curiosity so that she listened and stopped. Above the music of the organ there was the sound of a man's voice quarreling and the excited higher fussing of the monkey-man. She could hear the monkey chattering also. Then suddenly the organ stopped and the two different voices were loud and mad. F. Jasmine had reached the corner, and it was the corner by the Sears and Roebuck store; she passed the store slowly, then turned and faced a curious sight.

It was a narrow street that went downhill toward Front Avenue, blinding bright in the wild glare. There on the sidewalk was the monkey, the monkey-man, and a soldier holding out a whole fistful of dollar bills—it looked at the first glance like a hundred dollars. The soldier looked angry, and the monkey-man was pale and excited also. Their voices were quarreling and F. Jasmine gathered that the soldier was trying to buy the monkey. The monkey himself was crouched and shivering down on the sidewalk close to the brick wall of the Sears and Roebuck store. In spite of the hot day, he had on his little red coat with silver buttons and his little face, scared and desperate, had the look of someone who is just about to sneeze. Shivering and pitiful, he kept bowing at nobody and offering his cap into the air. He knew the furious voices were about him and he felt blamed.

F. Jasmine was standing near-by, trying to take in the commotion, listening and still. Then suddenly the soldier grabbed at the monkey's chain, but the monkey screamed, and before she knew what it was all about, the monkey had skittered up her leg and body and was huddled on her shoulder with his little monkey hands around her head. It happened in a flash, and she was so shocked she could not move. The voices stopped and, except for the monkey's jibbered scream, the street was silent. The soldier stood slack-jawed, surprised, still holding out the handful of dollar bills.

The monkey-man was the first to recover; he spoke to the monkey in a gentle voice, and in another second the monkey sprang from off her shoulder and landed on the organ which the monkey-man was carrying on his back. The two of them went away. They quickly hurried around the corner and at the last second, just as they turned, they both looked back with the same expression—reproaching and sly. F. Jasmine leaned against the brick wall, and she still felt the monkey on her shoulder and smelt his dusty, sour smell; she shivered. The soldier muttered until the pair of them were out of sight, and F. Jasmine noticed then that he was red-haired and the same soldier who had been in the Blue Moon. He stuffed the bills in his side pocket.

Exercise 3.1: Close Reading

In the blank space, write the *letter* of the choice that best completes the statement.

1. Frankie _____.

   (A) followed the monkey-man and the monkey as they left the soldier
   (B) had never seen the soldier before
   (C) used to follow the monkey-man and his monkey around town

2. In his treatment of the monkey, the monkey-man NEVER _____.

   (A) spoke gently to him
   (B) slapped him
   (C) pretended to slap him

3. The monkey was NOT supposed to _____.

   (A) bow to the audience
   (B) dance
   (C) reach out his hat to the monkey-man

4. F. Jasmine _____.

   (A) did not actually hear the soldier say that he wanted to buy the monkey
   (B) heard the monkey-man say that the offer was too low
   (C) heard the monkey-man say that he would not sell the monkey at any price

5. The monkey's behavior when the soldier grabbed at his chain shocked _____.

   (A) Frankie, the soldier, and the monkey-man
   (B) only Frankie
   (C) the soldier and Frankie, but not the monkey-man

6. There is no evidence that the monkey _____.

   (A) screamed   (B) sneezed   (C) shivered

7. Frankie had spent so much time with the monkey and the monkey-man that she
   _____.

   (A) became an unhappy child
   (B) got tired of watching them
   (C) looked sad when she was with them

8. The passage pays more attention to _____.

   (A) Frankie than to F. Jasmine
   (B) smells than to sounds
   (C) the monkey than to the monkey-man

LEARNING NEW WORDS

Line	Word	Meaning	Typical Use
4	**anxious** *(adj.)* 'aŋ(k)-shəs	1. fearful of what may happen; troubled; worried	Although she is favored to win, the champion is *anxious* about tomorrow's match.
		2. eager	At curtain-time, everyone was seated and *anxious* for the play to begin.
44–5	**commotion** *(n.)* kə-'mō-shən	noisy and confused excitement; disturbance; tumult	We will go home in mid-afternoon to avoid the *commotion* of the rush hour.
40	**desperate** *(adj.)* 'des-pə-rət	reckless because of loss of hope; hopeless	The firefighters reached the blaze in time to prevent the *desperate* tenant from jumping out the second-story window.
14	**exasperation** *(n.)* ig-ˌzas-pə-'rā-shən	extreme annoyance; irritation; anger	Dad's *exasperation* over the new car reached its peak when it had to be returned to the repair shop again.
15	**fascinate** *(v.)* 'fas-ən-ˌāt	attract very strongly; enchant by charming qualities	The circus has always been very popular because it *fascinates* both the old and the young.
36	**gather** *(v.)* 'gath-ər	1. conclude; guess	From the look on your face when you heard the news, I *gather* that you did not like it.
		2. bring together; collect	After completing the work, the plumbers *gathered* their tools and left.
11	**plead** *(v.)* 'plēd	argue earnestly; implore; appeal	When Jim wanted to drop out, his friends *pleaded* with him to remain in school.
60	**reproach** *(v.)* ri-'prōch	find fault with; rebuke; reprove; scold	The bus driver stopped the bus and *reproached* two of the pupils for their misconduct.
4	**resemble** *(v.)* ri-'zem-bəl	be like or similar to	People can easily tell I am Peter's brother because I *resemble* him.
	*(ant. **differ**)*		

Reading Selection 3: The Member of the Wedding

| 60 | **sly** *(adj.)* | tricky; cunning; stealthy | Arthur may slip past you when you least expect it; he is a *sly* opponent. |
| | 'slī | | |

APPLYING WHAT YOU HAVE LEARNED

Exercise 3.2: Sentence Completion

Which of the two choices correctly completes the sentence? Write the *letter* of your answer in the space provided.

1. The speaker was so ＿＿＿ that everyone was fascinated.

   A. interesting   B. uninteresting

2. Your reproaching look tells me that you are ＿＿＿ with me.

   A. dissatisfied   B. satisfied

3. It is useless to plead with anyone who has ＿＿＿ mind.

   A. an open   B. a closed

4. The commotion resulted from ＿＿＿ between the two neighbors.

   A. an agreement   B. a disagreement

5. You should not ＿＿＿ a person known to be sly in his dealings.

   A. trust   B. distrust

6. Did you gather that there would be a quiz today, or did ＿＿＿ that there would be one?

   A. you guess   B. the teacher announce

7. The desperate sailors ＿＿＿ to keep the ship afloat.

   A. were confident they would be able   B. threw the cargo overboard

8. The detective believes that these cases are ＿＿＿; they resemble each other.

   A. similar   B. different

9. Fred's exasperation was written all over his face; he looked very ＿＿＿.

   A. pleased   B. angry

10. At first, Emily was ＿＿＿ that her plan would work, but now she is anxious about it.

    A. confident   B. worried

Exercise 3.3: Definitions

Underline the choice that defines the italicized word.

1. closely *resembling:*   guessing, unlike, similar
2. *desperate* foe: eager, reckless, cunning
3. *fascinating* account: truthful, gloomy, enchanting
4. *plead* in vain: implore, blame, imagine
5. quite a *commotion:*   determination, tumult, surprise
6. without *exasperation:*   risk, delay, irritation
7. *gathered* my thoughts: doubted, collected, examined
8. *sly* manner: graceful, tricky, embarrassed
9. *anxious* parent: worried, angry, critical
10. gently *reproached:*   greeted, scolded, appealed

Exercise 3.4: Synonyms

For each italicized word or expression, write the best synonym from the vocabulary list at the bottom of the exercise.

_____   1. When he was tripped on purpose, Chuck could not hold back his *anger*.

_____   2. Running away from a problem is a *reckless* act.

_____   3. Her excuse *was similar to* the one we had heard many times before.

_____   4. We *appealed* for greater cooperation by all sides.

_____   5. The *cunning* bystander pretended not to be observing my work.

_____   6. From your expression, I *concluded* you were bored.

_____   7. The *fearful* patient inquired if the tooth could be saved.

_____   8. Stamp collecting *enchanted* me for a year or two, but then I gave it up.

_____   9. Eric was *reproved* for his frequent interruptions.

_____   10. What caused the *disturbance?*

Vocabulary List

resembled	reproached
sly	commotion
fascinated	exasperation
anxious	gathered
pleaded	desperate

Each word in bold type is a *root*. The words below it are its *derivatives*.

anxious *(adj.)*   She is *anxious* about the results.

anxiously *(adv.)*   She is *anxiously* awaiting the results.

anxiety *(n.)*   She is awaiting the results with *anxiety*.

desperate *(adj.)*   Our team was *desperate*.

desperately *(adv.)*   Our team tried *desperately* to tie the score.

desperation *(n.)*   In *desperation*, we asked for "time out."

despair *(n.)*   In *despair*, we tried a risky play.

exasperate *(v.)*   Traffic tie-ups *exasperate* us.

exasperating *(adj.)*   Traffic jams are *exasperating*.

exasperation *(n.)*   With each moment of delay, my *exasperation* increased.

fascinate *(v.)*   Why do snakes *fascinate* you?

fascinating *(adj.)*   Why do you find snakes so *fascinating?*

fascination *(n.)*   What *fascination* do you find in snakes?

plead *(v.)*   The candidate *pleaded* for our support.

plea *(n.)*   The candidate made a *plea* for our support.

reproach *(n.)*   I did not deserve your *reproach*.

reproaching *(adj.)*   You should not have spoken to me in a *reproaching* voice.

reproachingly *(adv.)*   You should not have spoken to me *reproachingly*.

reproach *(v.)*   You should not have *reproached* me.

resemble *(v.)*   You *resemble* your father.

resemblance *(n.)*   There is a strong *resemblance* between you and your father.

sly *(adj.)*   The *sly* fox outsmarted the hunters.

slyly *(adv.)*   The fox *slyly* outwitted the hunters.

slyness *(n.)*   By his *slyness*, the fox escaped from the hunters.

Exercise 3.5: Roots and Derivatives

Fill each blank below with the root or derivative just listed that best completes the sentence.

1. As hope fades, _____ sets in.

2. The lawyer made a passionate _____ for the release of his client.

3. You say the two problems are alike, but I fail to see the _____.

4. Mother shook a finger at me _____ when I reached for the dessert too soon.

5. Your _____ caught me by surprise. I never suspected you could be so cunning.

6. The program enchanted the younger children, but it had no _____ for us.

7. Everyone who received a sled for Christmas was looking forward _____ to the first snowfall.

8. You can rebuke someone without words by using a look of _____.

9. Stop worrying; _____ is bad for your health.

10. I saw that Fred was annoyed by our questioning and that further inquiries would surely _____ him.

IMPROVING YOUR SPELLING: ADDING THE SUFFIX -*ION*

1. By adding the suffix **-ion,** meaning "act or result of," we may change many verbs to nouns:

Verb	*Suffix*		*Noun*
fascinate	+ -ion	=	fascination

(act or result of fascinating)

(*a*) We drop the **e** in *fascinate* because **-ion** begins with a *vowel.*

| But: | attract | + -ion | = | attraction |

(act or result of attracting)

(*b*) We add **-ion** directly because *attract* ends in **t,** a *consonant.*

Exercise 3.6: Changing Verbs to Nouns

Change the following verbs to nouns by adding **-ion.** Follow the sample given below.

	Verb	*Noun*
	graduate	**graduation**
1.	humiliate	_____
2.	promote	_____
3.	appreciate	_____
4.	invent	_____
5.	operate	_____
6.	express	_____
7.	abbreviate	_____
8.	select	_____
9.	impress	_____
10.	separate	_____

2. By dropping the suffix **-ion,** we may change nouns to verbs:

Noun	*Suffix*		*Verb*
confession	− -ion	=	confess
attraction	− -ion	=	attract

Caution: If an **e** was dropped when **-ion** was added, put back that **e** when **-ion** is dropped. Study the following:

fascination − -ion + e = fascinate
humiliation − -ion + e = humiliate

Exercise 3.7: Changing Nouns to Verbs

Change the following nouns to verbs by dropping **-ion.** Follow the sample given below.

	Noun	*Verb*
	education	**educate**
1.	irritation	_____
2.	discussion	_____
3.	contribution	_____
4.	investigation	_____
5.	adoption	_____
6.	hesitation	_____
7.	construction	_____

8. pollution _____

9. regulation _____

10. depression _____

Exercise 3.8: Wordbuilding With *-ED, -ER, -ING,* and *-ION*

Fill each blank with a word formed by adding one of the above suffixes to the word in parentheses. The first blank has been filled as a sample.

1. Squirrels can be __**fascinating**__ . (*fascinate*)

2. A good _____ pays close attention. *(observe)*

3. The captives _____ for their freedom. *(plead)*

4. What caused the _____? *(irritate)*

5. Why are you _____ me? *(reproach)*

6. The crime _____ the nation. *(horrify)*

7. Their bad manners filled me with _____ . *(loathe)*

8. You _____ me yesterday. *(exasperate)*

9. They are still _____ . *(argue)*

10. Yesterday's sale _____ a riot. *(resemble)*

USING ADJECTIVES RATHER THAN ADVERBS AFTER CERTAIN VERBS

Notice that Carson McCullers says:

"The soldier looked angry." (not *angrily*)

In this sentence, "looked" has about the same meaning as "was"; essentially, the author is saying:

"The soldier *was* angry."

Therefore, in the sentence "The soldier looked *(was)* angry," the adjective *angry* describes the noun *soldier:* angry soldier.

We also say:

The food tasted *(was)* delicious. (not *deliciously*)

The adjective *delicious* describes the noun *food:* delicious food.

My shoe feels *(is)* tight. (not *tightly*)

The adjective *tight* describes the noun *shoe:* tight shoe.

Use an adjective instead of an adverb after the following verbs when they have the meaning of *is, are, was, were,* or any other part of the verb *to be.*

look	feel	taste	remain
seem	smell	become	stay
appear	sound	grow	turn

Exercise 3.9: Adjective or Adverb

Fill each blank with the correct choice.

1. The plan seems _____. *(interesting* or *interestingly)*

2. Your carelessness exasperates me _____. *(terrible* or *terribly)*

3. Romeo speaks _____ to Juliet in the balcony scene. *(passionate* or *passionately)*

4. Your voice sounded _____ on the telephone. *(strange* or *strangely)*

5. This plastic product resembles wood _____. *(close* or *closely)*

6. A stranger _____ inquired for directions. *(polite* or *politely)*

7. Doesn't this material feel _____? *(soft* or *softly)*

8. She looks _____. *(beautiful* or *beautifully)*

9. The cheese does not taste _____. *(fresh* or *freshly)*

10. Let the air out _____. *(gradual* or *gradually)*

IMPROVING YOUR COMPOSITION SKILLS: DESCRIPTION

Carson McCullers offers a fine example of how to describe a mistake.

> **"The monkey, in fact, was nearly always wrong; after he danced to the organ tune, he was supposed to take off his darling little cap and pass it around to the audience, but likely as not he would get mixed up and bow and reach out his cap to the monkey-man, and not the audience."**

Exercise 3.10: Describing a Mistake

Describe how someone got mixed up and made a mistake. Present your material in the order that Carson McCullers used.

First tell who made the mistake.
Next explain what he, she, or it was supposed to do.
Then describe what he, she, or it actually did.

Sample Answer:

A MISTAKE

Henry was supposed to take the downtown train to the hotel where the party was being held, but he got mixed up and boarded an uptown train that took him in the direction of the Bronx Zoo.

Below, write your description of a mistake.

_____

_____

_____

_____

_____

_____

_____

_____

_____

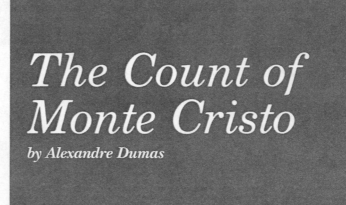

The Count of Monte Cristo

by Alexandre Dumas

A crowd of French citizens has gathered to watch the entry of a merchant ship into Marseilles harbor. Something strange in the manner of the vessel's approach excites their curiosity. Let us find out what has happened.

Meanwhile the vessel drew on, and was approaching the harbor under topsails, jib, and foresail, but so slowly and with such an air of melancholy that the spectators, always ready to sense misfortune, began to ask one another what ill-luck had over-
5 taken those on board. However, those experienced in navigation soon saw that if there had been any ill-luck, the ship had not been the sufferer, for she advanced in perfect condition and under skilful handling; the anchor was ready to be dropped, the bowsprit shrouds loose. Beside the pilot, who was steering the *Pharaon*
10 through the narrow entrance to the port, there stood a young man, quick of gesture and keen of eye, who watched every movement of the ship while repeating each of the pilot's orders.

The vague anxiety that prevailed among the crowd affected one of the spectators so much that he could not wait until the ship
15 reached the port; jumping into a small boat, he ordered the boatman to row him alongside the *Pharaon*, which he reached opposite the creek of La Réserve.

On seeing this man approach, the young sailor left his post beside the pilot, and, hat in hand, leant over the ship's bulwarks.
20 He was a tall, lithe young man of about twenty years of age, with fine dark eyes and hair as black as ebony; his whole manner bespoke that air of calm resolution peculiar to those who, from their childhood, have been accustomed to face danger.

"Ah, is that you, Dantès!" cried the man in the boat. "You are
looking pretty gloomy on board. What has happened?"

"A great misfortune, Monsieur Morrel," replied the young
man, "a great misfortune, especially for me! We lost our brave
Captain Leclère off Civita Vecchia."

"What happened to him?" asked the shipowner. "What has
happened to our worthy captain?"

"He died of brain-fever in dreadful agony. Alas, monsieur, the
whole thing was most unexpected. After a long conversation with
the harbormaster, Captain Leclère left Naples in a great state of
agitation. In twenty-four hours he was in high fever, and died
three days afterwards. We performed the usual burial service. He
is now at rest off the Isle of El Giglio, sewn up in his hammock,
with a thirty-six-pounder shot at his head and another at his heels.
We have brought home his sword and his cross of honor to his
widow. But was it worth his while," added the young man, with
a sad smile, "to wage war against the English for ten long years
only to die in his bed like everybody else?"

"Well, well, Monsieur Edmond," replied the owner, who
appeared more comforted with every moment, "we are all mortal,
and the old must make way for the young; otherwise there would
be no promotion."

Line 20. *lithe:* effortlessly graceful

Line 21. *ebony:* hard, heavy, black wood

UNDERSTANDING THE SELECTION

Exercise 4.1: Close Reading

In the blank space, write the *letter* of the choice that best completes the statement.

1. The spectators felt that a misfortune had occurred because the *Pharaon* _C_ .

    (A) appeared to be damaged
    (B) required assistance to enter the harbor
    (C) approached so very, very gradually

2. Monsieur Morrel's object in having a boatman row him to the *Pharaon* was to _C_ .

    (A) learn as quickly as possible what had happened
    (B) inspect the damage to the vessel
    (C) help pilot the vessel into port

3. Edmond Dantès has an acute sense of _A_ .

    (A) sight
    (B) humor
    (C) hearing

4. The statement about the late Captain Leclère that is NOT true is _A_ .

    (A) he died comfortably
    (B) he fought the English for ten years
    (C) he appeared to be profoundly vexed after his conversation with the Naples harbormaster

5. The *Pharaon* depended on _C_ for its sailing power.

    (A) steam
    (B) oil
    (C) wind

6. The *Pharaon's* movements into port were determined by _A_ .

    (A) the pilot and Dantès
    (B) the pilot only
    (C) Dantès only

7. Morrel _B_ .

    (A) was slow to recover from the news of the captain's death
    (B) did not board the *Pharaon*
    (C) seems to be in poor physical condition

8. The selection suggests that _A_ .

    (A) Leclère received no recognition for his war services
    (B) Morrel will be unable to continue in business
    (C) Dantès is in line for a promotion

LEARNING NEW WORDS

Line	Word	Meaning	Typical Use
34	**agitation** *(n.)* ˌaj-ə-ˈtā-shən	violent upset; excited or disturbed condition	The physician ended the mother's *agitation* by assuring her that her child would soon be well.
		(ant. **calmness***)*	I was afraid Bill would be greatly upset in learning of the damage to his car, but he received the news with *calmness*.
31	**agony** *(n.)* ˈag-ə-nē	intense pain of mind or body; anguish; torture	My sunburn itched so very painfully that I was in *agony*.
11	**gesture** *(n.)* ˈjes-chər	hand, arm, or body motion to help express an idea	By a *gesture*, the traffic officer ordered the motorist to pull over to the curb.

25	**gloomy** *(adj.)* 'glü-mē	1. dark; dim; partially or totally dark *(ant.* **brilliant**) 2. in low spirits; sad; melancholy *(ant.* **cheerful**)	We emerged from the *gloomy* tunnel into the bright sunshine. Broadway at night is *brilliant* with electric lights. You, too, would feel *gloomy* if your bicycle had been stolen.
3	**melancholy** *(n.)* 'mel-ən-ˌkäl-ē	low spirits; sadness; dejection; gloom *(ant.* **exhilaration**)	The good news lifted me out of my *melancholy*. One of the teams will leave the field in the gloom of defeat, and the other in the *exhilaration* of victory.
43	**mortal** *(adj.)* 'mȯrt-ᵊl	1. subject to death; certain to die sometime *(ant.* **immortal**) 2. fatal; causing death; deadly	All living things are *mortal*. According to Greek legend, the gods and goddesses cannot die; they are *immortal*. In his victory at Trafalgar, Nelson suffered a *mortal* wound.
5	**navigation** *(n.)* ˌnav-ə-'gā-shən	art of sailing a ship, airplane, etc.	Mathematics is very important in the *navigation* of a space vehicle.
22	**resolution** *(n.)* ˌrez-ə-'lü-shən	determination; firmness of resolve	Nothing could shake Joan of Arc from her *resolution* to lead the French to victory over the English invaders.
14	**spectator** *(n.)* 'spek-ˌtāt-ər	person who looks on or watches, without taking part; onlooker	Because of his injury, Keith could not play, but he nevertheless attended the game as a *spectator*.
13	**vague** *(adj.)* 'vāg	not clear; indefinite *(ant.* **definite, specific**)	Instead of a definite "yes" or "no" answer, all we got was a *vague* "maybe." I told Dad I would be back late, and when he asked me to be more *specific (definite)*, I said I would be home by 12:15.

Exercise 4.2: Sentence Completion

Which of the two choices correctly completes the sentence? Write the *letter* of your answer in the space provided.

1. Failure usually causes ____, but success brings with it a feeling of ____.

   A. exhilaration   B. melancholy

2. Did you ____ the program, or were you just a spectator?

   A. participate in   B. watch

3. Try to be ____. If you are ____, no one will know what you are talking about.

   A. vague   B. definite

4. Most patients enter the dentist's office ____ and depart ____.

   A. cheerfully   B. gloomily

5. In fairy tales, the gods and goddesses are ____, but ordinary people are mortal.

   A. not supposed to work   B. supposed to live forever

6. Navigation is difficult when maps are ____ or not available.

   A. indefinite   B. specific

7. Not to awaken the child, the parents tried to communicate with each other by ____.

   A. word of mouth   B. gesture

8. The family's agony ____ when they were told that their dog would recover from his injuries.

   A. increased   B. decreased

9. The pilot's ____ made the passengers less anxious.

   A. agitation   B. calmness

10. Barbara's ____ supporters gradually became ____ as it grew clear that she would lose the election.

    A. melancholy   B. joyous

Exercise 4.3: Definitions

Each expression below defines a word that can be found in the vocabulary list at the bottom of the exercise. Enter that word in the space provided.

_____ 1. low spirits

_____ 2. art of sailing

_____ 3. hand, arm, or body motion

_____ 4. not clear

_____ 5. person who looks on

_____ 6. partially or totally dark

_____ 7. intense pain of mind or body

_____ 8. firmness of resolve

_____ 9. excited or disturbed condition

_____ 10. subject to death

Vocabulary List

gesture	navigation
spectator	mortal
agony	melancholy
gloomy	resolution
agitation	vague

Exercise 4.4: Synonyms and Antonyms

Fill in the blanks with the required synonyms or antonyms, selecting them from the vocabulary list at the right.

Vocabulary List

_____ 1. synonym for *sadness*   onlooker

_____ 2. antonym for *calmness*   brilliant

_____ 3. synonym for *resolution*   exhilaration

_____ 4. antonym for *dim*   melancholy

_____ 5. synonym for *deadly*   agony

_____ 6. antonym for *dejection*   fatal

_____ 7. synonym for *spectator*   agitation

_____ 8. antonym for *vague*   specific

_____ 9. synonym for *anguish*   navigation

_____ 10. synonym for *sailing*   determination

LEARNING SOME ROOTS AND DERIVATIVES

Each word in bold type is a **root**. The words below it are its **derivatives**.

agitate *(v.)*   What is *agitating* you?

agitation *(n.)*   What is the cause of your *agitation?*

gesture *(n.)*   By a *gesture,* the crossing guard brought traffic to a halt.

gesture *(v.)*   The crossing guard *gestured* for traffic to halt.

gloom *(n.)*   After hearing the news, we left in *gloom.*

gloomy *(adj.)*   We were *gloomy* when we heard the news.

gloomily *(adv.)*   After hearing the news, we departed *gloomily.*

melancholy *(n.)*   You passed. You have no reason for *melancholy.*

melancholy *(adj.)*   You passed. You have no reason to be *melancholy.*

mortal *(adj.)*   Fortunately the injury was not *mortal.*

mortally *(adv.)*   Fortunately he was not *mortally* injured.

navigate *(v.)*   It is difficult to *navigate* in a storm.

navigation *(n.)*   In a storm, *navigation* is difficult.

navigator *(n.)*   A storm creates difficulties for a *navigator.*

resolute *(adj.)*   Be *resolute.* Don't give up.

resolutely *(adv.)*   Stick *resolutely* to your goal.

resolution *(n.)*   Don't let anything sway you from your *resolution* to succeed.

vague *(adj.)*   Her replies were *vague.*

vaguely *(adv.)*   She answered *vaguely.*

vagueness *(n.)*   The *vagueness* of her answers made it hard to get a clear idea of what had happened.

Exercise 4.5: Roots and Derivatives

Fill each blank below with the root or derivative just listed that best completes the sentence.

1. The fog made it difficult to _____ the vessel into port.

2. Abraham Lincoln was _____ wounded by an assassin.

3. Don't say anything; just _____ your approval by a nod.

4. As a true friend, you have always supported me and stood _____ by my side.

5. The spectator described the incident so _____ that I could form no definite idea of what had happened.

6. The meeting opened _____ because we had just received bad news.

7. Why do you get so violently upset if you have to wait for me? A delay of a minute or or two should not _____ you.

8. Amelia Earhart's distinguished achievements in aviation show that she was an excellent _____ .

9. Someone who is _____ is not easily discouraged.

10. There is no reason for melancholy. Don't look so _____ .

IMPROVING YOUR SPELLING: THE SUFFIX -*LY*

1. To change an adjective to an adverb, we usually add **-ly.**

    vague + ly = vaguely
    mortal + ly = mortally

2. If the adjective ends in **-y,** change the **y** to **i** before adding **-ly.**

    happy + ly = happily

    Exceptions: slyly, shyly, dryly.

3. If the adjective ends in **-ic,** add **al** plus **-ly.**

    specific + al + ly = specifically

4. If the adjective ends in a consonant plus **le**—as in *able, probable, ample, gentle,* etc.—drop the **le** and add **-ly.**

    probable − le + ly = probably

Exercise 4.6: Changing Adjectives to Adverbs
Enter the required adverbs.

	Adjective	*Adverb*
1.	cheerful	_____
2.	immortal	_____

3. definite   _____

4. specific   _____

5. desperate   _____

6. reckless   _____

7. gloomy   _____

8. brilliant   _____

9. probable   _____

10. conceivable   _____

11. fatal   _____

12. clumsy   _____

13. acute   _____

14. unhappy   _____

15. profound   _____

16. sly   _____

17. joyous   _____

18. gentle   _____

19. easy   _____

20. able   _____

Exercise 4.7: Changing Adverbs to Adjectives

Enter the required adjectives.

Adverb	*Adjective*
1. indefinitely	_____
2. mortally	_____
3. gloomily	_____
4. probably	_____
5. resolutely	_____
6. slyly	_____
7. fatally	_____
8. conceivably	_____
9. anxiously	_____
10. gradually	_____
11. specifically	_____
12. passionately	_____

13. unhappily _____

14. shyly _____

15. tragically _____

16. clumsily _____

17. horribly _____

18. naturally _____

19. democratically _____

20. ably _____

Exercise 4.8:   Using Adjectives and Adverbs

Insert the adjective or adverb needed in column B.

Column A	*Column B*
1. The sun rose *brilliantly.*	It was a _____ sunrise.
2. It was *fortunate* I had my key.	_____, I had my key.
3. I *vaguely* remember the place.	I have a _____ memory of the place.
4. Mark leaped for the ball *clumsily.*	Mark made a _____ leap for the ball.
5. We got a *cheerful* welcome.	We were _____ welcomed.
6. The story has a *gloomy* ending.	The story ends _____.
7. Clean air is *critically* important.	Clean air is of _____ importance.
8. Magellan suffered a *mortal* wound.	Magellan was _____ wounded.
9. Sue glanced at me *reproachingly.*	Sue gave me a _____ glance.
10. You received *specific* instructions to let nobody in.	You were _____ instructed to let nobody in.

1. The word **affect** is a *verb,* meaning **"to influence."**

   Alexandre Dumas says:

   > "The vague anxiety that prevailed among the crowd *affected* (influenced) one of the spectators so much that he could not wait until the ship reached the port."

   A further example:

   > Absence may *affect* (influence) your mark.

2. The word **effect** is most often a *noun,* meaning **"result."**

   > One *effect* (result) of absence may be a lower mark.

   > What is the *effect* (result) of going without sleep?

   To sum up, if the sentence calls for a verb meaning "to influence," use **affect.** If it calls for a noun meaning "result," use **effect.**

Exercise 4.9: *Affect* or *Effect?*

SAMPLE: What would be the **effect** of my resigning?

SAMPLE: Do not let these small problems **affect** you.

1. Tobacco and drugs _____ the lives of countless persons.

2. The candidate's speech did not _____ my vote.

3. So far my efforts have produced no observable _____ .

4. Drinking is known to _____ a driver's judgment.

5. The new traffic light will have the _____ of reducing accidents.

6. Does advertising _____ you?

7. The _____ of the experiment did not surprise me.

8. You should not let her remark _____ you.

9. One _____ of the reduction in funds is that we will have fewer teams.

10. The mother's plea did not seem to _____ her son's decision.

To write concisely is to express one's ideas in no more words than necessary.

> *Question:* How can the following be expressed more concisely?
>
> Those who had been captured were in low spirits.
>
> *Answer:* **The captives were gloomy.**

Exercise 4.10: Concise Writing

Rewrite each of the following sentences, using no more than four words. The first sentence has been rewritten as a sample.

1. People sometimes use hand, arm, or body motions to help express what they want to say.

   People sometimes use gestures.
   _____

2. The fame that Washington achieved by his deeds will last for ever and ever.

   _____

3. The answer that she gave did not convey a clear idea.

   _____

4. Every single person in this whole wide world is sure to die at some time or other.

   _____

5. We interviewed someone who had been watching from the sidelines without actually taking part in what was going on.

   _____

Review I.1: Vocabulary and Spelling

Fill in the missing letters of the *Word*. (Each space stands for one missing letter.) Then write the *Complete Word* in the blank space.

Definition	Word	Complete Word
1. alarmed; greatly troubled	DISM __ __ ED	_____
2. sailing	NAV __ __ __ __ ING	_____
3. bird of prey	__ __ __ TURE	_____
4. imaginable	CONC __ __ __ ABLE	_____
5. prisoner	__ __ __ TIVE	_____
6. act of annoying	VEX __ __ ION	_____
7. strong disgust	LO __ __ __ ING	_____
8. stealthily; cunningly	S __ __ LY	_____
9. determination	RESO __ __ __ ION	_____
10. one who watches	OBS __ __ __ ER	_____
11. reckless because of loss of hope	DES __ __ __ ATE	_____
12. act of attracting very strongly	FAS __ __ __ ATION	_____
13. little by little	GRAD __ __ __	_____
14. strong, overpowering feeling	PAS __ __ __ __	_____
15. extreme annoyance	EXAS __ __ __ __ TION	_____
16. advice	COUN __ __ __	_____
17. meeting; conference	__ __ __ __ CIL	_____
18. anguish; torture	__ __ ONY	_____
19. purpose; aim	OB __ __ __ __	_____
20. dislike; antipathy	AVER __ __ __ __	_____

Review I.2: Synonyms

To each line, add a word that has the *same meaning* as the first two words on the line. Choose your words from the vocabulary list.

Vocabulary List

 1. sad; dejected _____

 2. blaming; rebuking _____

 3. vaguely; unclearly _____

 4. purpose; aim _____

 5. pride-lowering; mortifying _____

 6. deadly; fatal _____

 7. irritation; exasperation _____

 8. watcher; observer _____

 9. disturbance; commotion _____

10. rarely; seldom _____

infrequently

anger

mortal

melancholy

reproaching

tumult

indefinitely

humiliating

spectator

object

Review I.3: Antonyms

For each italicized word in column A, write the best *antonym* from column B.

Column A / *Column B*

_____ 1. *dull* pain   differed

_____ 2. *resembled* greatly specific

_____ 3. *vexed* her parents solid

_____ 4. *melancholy* song   profound

_____ 5. *brilliant* lighting joyous

_____ 6. *hollow* log   acute

_____ 7. *vague* details   calmness

_____ 8. *seldom* heard   often

_____ 9. with obvious *agitation* pleased

_____ 10. *shallow* observer   gloomy

Review I.4: Wordbuilding With Suffixes

Fill each blank with a word formed by adding one of the following suffixes to the word in parentheses. The first statement has been completed as a sample.

-ABLE, -ATION, -ED, -ER, -ION, -LY

1. A person may become ill from __vexation__. *(vex)*

2. We didn't like the film; we _____ it. *(loathe)*

3. The defenders _____ refused to surrender. *(resolute)*

4. I tried by every means _____ to solve the problem. *(conceive)*

5. Many of us learn by _____. *(observe)*

6. The _____ received a polite reply. *(inquire)*

7. Further delay will only increase their _____. *(exasperate)*

8. Josh _____ me for my stubbornness. *(reproach)*

9. I find a _____ in magic shows. *(fascinate)*

10. She is _____ waiting for her turn. *(anxious)*

Review I.5: Sentence Completion

Complete each sentence below with the most appropriate word from the following vocabulary list:

Vocabulary List

vague	council	humiliating
fascinated	mortal	captive
seldom	melancholy	counsel
gathered	gesture	profound

1. Why are you _____ when everyone else is cheerful?

2. Before making up your mind, ask your friends for their _____.

3. By a _____, Ms. Davis signaled Eric to come up to her desk.

4. The wound was very serious, but fortunately not _____.

5. Most of the time Fred is with friends; you _____ see him alone.

6. Your report is too _____; make it more specific.

7. Since the door was locked and the lights were out, I _____ that you were not at home.

8. Our family wishes to express its _____ thanks for your wonderful help in the emergency.

9. It was _____ for him to be knocked down by a little-known fighter.

10. At first her ideas _____ us, but we soon grew tired of them.

Review I.6: Roots and Derivatives

On lines B and C, write the required forms of the italicized word on line A.

1. A. The homework was a *vexing* problem.

   B. The homework _____ me.

   C. The homework caused me _____.

2. A. He is *desperately* in debt.

   B. He is _____ over his debts.

   C. His debts are driving him to _____.

3. A. Your *sly* foe outwitted you.

   B. Your foe _____ outwitted you.

   C. By _____ your foe outwitted you.

4. A. She spoke in a *pleading* voice.

   B. She made a _____.

   C. She _____.

5. A. Will the eclipse be *observable* in our area?

   B. Will we be able to _____ the eclipse?

   C. Can the eclipse be _____ in our area?

6. A. They are *exasperating*.

   B. They drove us to _____.

   C. They _____ us.

7. A. Are you a good *navigator*?

   B. Are you skilled in _____?

   C. Do you know how to _____?

8. A. Who *inquired*?

   B. Who made the _____?

   C. Who was the _____?

9. A. Such an idea is *inconceivable*.

   B. We cannot _____ of such an idea.

   C. Such an idea is not _____.

10. A. *Gloom* descended on the losers as they left the field.

    B. The losers _____ left the field.

    C. The _____ losers left the field.

11. A. Our arguments were *dispassionate.*

   B. Our arguments were free from _____.

   C. Our arguments were not _____.

12. A. Injustice is *loathsome* to me.

   B. I _____ injustice.

   C. I have a _____ for injustice.

13. A. Avoid *vagueness* in giving directions.

   B. Do not give directions _____.

   C. Don't be _____ in giving directions.

14. A. They looked at me in a *reproaching* way.

   B. They gave me a look of _____.

   C. They _____ me by their look.

15. A. Are you *anxious* about tomorrow's game?

   B. Does the thought of tomorrow's game fill you with _____?

   C. Are you _____ concerned about tomorrow's game?

16. A. It is a play of deep *fascination.*

   B. It is a deeply _____ play.

   C. The play will _____ you deeply.

17. A. The party members *resolutely* defended their leader.

   B. The party members showed _____ in defending their leader.

   C. The party members were _____ in the defense of their leader.

18. A. What do you find so *dismaying?*

   B. Why are you _____?

   C. What reason is there for _____?

19. A. Your remark profoundly *humiliated* me.

   B. Your remark caused me profound _____.

   C. I found your remark profoundly _____.

20. A. Try to overcome your *shyness.*

   B. Don't behave so _____.

   C. Try not to be so _____.

Review I.7: Concise Writing

Suggest two ways to get rid of the repetition in each of the following statements. The first statement has been rewritten *twice* as a sample.

1. The place has no charm for me, but my friends find it charming.

   HINT. One way is to get rid of **charming:**

   a. The place has no charm for me, but my friends find it **fascinating.**

   HINT. Another way is to get rid of **charm:**

   b. The place has no **fascination** for me, but my friends find it charming.

2. Joe loathes work, so the thought of getting a job fills him with loathing.

   a. _____

   b. _____

3. Her exasperation with the puppy grew. Everything it did exasperated her.

   a. _____

   b. _____

4. There is an urgent labor shortage. Additional workers are urgently needed.

   a. _____

   b. _____

5. We had hoped to escape observation, but someone observed us leaving.

   a. _____

   b. _____

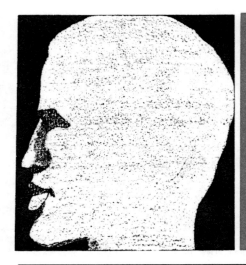

Crispus Attucks, Martyr for American Independence

by Langston Hughes

Five years before the outbreak of the Revolutionary War, there occurred an event known as the Boston Massacre. It was caused by the bad feeling between the people of Boston and the British troops that had been sent to their city. Here is an account of that event.

Near the waterfront, in the crowd milling about between Dock Square and Long Wharf, a gigantic man of color stood out above almost everyone's head. A mulatto of light complexion then in his forties, his name was Crispus Attucks. He was a seaman but lately
5 discharged from a whaling vessel, and little is known about his life except that in his youth Attucks had been a runaway slave. Twenty years before that fateful night of moonlight and blood this advertisement had thrice appeared in the *Boston Gazette:*

Ran away from his Master, *William Brown* of Framingham, on
10 the 30th of Sept. last, a Mulatto Fellow, about 27 Years of Age, named Crispus, 6 Feet two inches high, short curl'd hair, his Knees nearer together than common; had on a light colour'd Bearskin Coat, plain brown fustian Jacket, or brown all-Wool one, new Buckskin Breeches, blue Yarn Stocking, and a check'd woolen
15 Shirt. Whoever shall take up said Run-away, and convey him to his abovesaid Master, shall have ten pounds, old Tenor Reward, and all necessary Charges paid. And all Masters of Vessels and others are hereby caution'd against concealing or carrying off said Servant on Penalty of the Law.

20   *Boston, October 2, 1750.*

But, so far as is known, in spite of the repetitions of this ad, William Brown of Framingham never recovered his runaway slave. Crispus Attucks had taken to the high seas as a sailor. So on that night of March 5, 1770, with snow on the ground and a bright moon in the sky, he felt himself a free man allied with the citizens of Boston in their indignation that freedom to run their own affairs should be denied them by the English.

About nine o'clock that night, taunted by youngsters, a sentinel had knocked a boy down in front of the Custom House. Whereupon, other boys began to throw snowballs at the Red Coat as a crowd of men came running to the scene. Crying for help, the sentinel ran up the steps of the Custom House while someone else of his company rushed to call out the guard. A group of British privates officered by Captain Preston trotted doublequick up King Street and were met by a crowd of citizens that included the towering Crispus Attucks, and these were armed with sticks and stones. As the soldiers ran with drawn bayonets through the street, they were pelted by chunks of ice and handfuls of snow. Then the Red Coats encountered this group of men with stones and sticks in their hands. Crispus Attucks cried, "The way to get rid of these soldiers is to attack the main guard! Strike at the root! This is the nest!" And the men began to use their crude weapons against the well armed British.

Then the guns went off. An order to fire had been given. The very first shot killed Crispus Attucks. Maybe, being tall and Negro, he was the most conspicuous person in the crowd. At any rate, Attucks was the first man to lose his life in the cause of American freedom, pierced by a British bullet in the streets of Boston.

To his aid came Samuel Gray, a white man. And Gray, too, on the instant was shot dead. The next to fall was a sailor, James Caldwell. Then Patrick Carr and a boy of only seventeen, Samuel Maverick, gravely wounded, tumbled to the cobblestones. The boy died the next morning and Carr nine days later. A half dozen others were shot, but not fatally.

Line 3. *mulatto:* person of mixed black and white ancestry

Line 25. *allied with:* on the side of

Line 38. *pelted:* struck

UNDERSTANDING THE SELECTION

Exercise 5.1: Close Reading

In the blank space, write the *letter* of the choice that best completes the statement or answers the question.

1. The selection states that we do not know much about _____.

   (A) the events of March 5, 1770
   (B) Crispus Attucks
   (C) William Brown

2. Altogether, _____ persons were killed when the soldiers fired into the crowd.

   (A) eleven
   (B) six
   (C) five

3. On the night of March 5, 1770 _____.

   (A) it was snowing
   (B) the crowd showed remarkable self-control
   (C) both the crowd and the soldiers lost their tempers

4. Crispus Attucks _____.

   (A) tried to calm the crowd
   (B) urged the crowd to attack the soldiers
   (C) had no arms of any kind

5. When he lost his life, Crispus Attucks was about _____ years old.

   (A) forty-seven
   (B) twenty
   (C) twenty-seven

6. The selection suggests that William Brown _____.

   (A) hesitated for several days before placing his ad in the *Boston Gazette*
   (B) was not entirely sure of what Crispus Attucks was wearing at the time of his disappearance
   (C) did not have the law on his side in his attempt to recover Crispus Attucks

7. Of those who were shot by the Red Coats, _____.

   (A) one was a sailor
   (B) two died at the scene
   (C) six recovered

8. Which of the following statements about Crispus Attucks is NOT supported by the selection? _____

   (A) He was the tallest person in the crowd.
   (B) He had a passion for freedom.
   (C) He felt that the Bostonians had the right to manage their own affairs.

Line	Word	Meaning	Typical Use
18	**conceal** *(v.)* kən-'sēl	hide; place out of sight	Nancy *concealed* her diary in a secret place where her sister would be unlikely to find it.
		(ant. **display***)*	People, as a rule, do not *display* their faults but tend to keep them secret.
		(ant. **expose***)*	In speaking to Mara, be careful not to *expose* the surprise party we are planning for her.
46	**conspicuous** *(adj.)* kən-'spik-yə-wəs	easily seen; attracting attention; striking	You will have no trouble recognizing my cousin Andy. His flaming red hair makes him *conspicuous*.
		(ant. **concealed, inconspicuous***)*	As I wanted to be *inconspicuous,* I retired to the background where I would not attract too much attention.
27	**deny** *(v.)* di-'nī	1. refuse	The applicant was *denied* a driver's license because of failing the road test.
		2. declare not to be true	There was a rumor that we would be dismissed early on Friday, but our teacher *denied* it.
		(ant. **confirm***)*	Dr. Miller immediately thought I had fractured the arm, and the X-rays that were taken *confirmed* his opinion.
2	**gigantic** *(adj.)* jī-'gan-tik	greater in size than usual; huge; like a giant	The *gigantic* redwood trees along the coast of California are from 100 to 340 feet tall.
53	**gravely** *(adv.)* 'grāv-lē	in a grave (serious) manner; seriously	The workman was so *gravely* injured that at first it seemed he would not recover.

26	**indignation** (*n.*) ˌin-dig-ˈnā-shən	anger aroused by something unjust, unworthy, or mean; righteous anger	Many students, parents, and teachers have expressed their *indignation* at the proposal to do away with clubs and teams.
4	**lately** (*adv.*) ˈlāt-lē	in the near past; recently	Joan has been ill *lately;* she has not been to school in recent days.
22	**recover** (*v.*) ri-ˈkəv-ər	1. get back; regain	The ex-champion is seeking a return match in an attempt to *recover* the title.
		2. regain health; get well	Larry *recovered* from his cold and returned to work after a day's absence.
28–9	**sentinel** (*n.*) ˈsent-ən-əl	one who watches or guards; sentry	A *sentinel* was posted day and night outside the command post.
28	**taunt** (*v.*) ˈtȯnt	jeer at; reproach; challenge in a mocking or insulting manner	Some of the boys *taunted* Jeff with cries of "coward" and "chicken," but he refused to jump from the high diving board.

APPLYING WHAT YOU HAVE LEARNED

Exercise 5.2: Sentence Completion

Which of the two choices correctly completes the sentence? Write the *letter* of your answer in the space provided.

1. I aroused my brother's indignation by _____ my promise.

   A. breaking   B. keeping

2. Cheryl was denied admission because _____.

   A. there were plenty of seats   B. she had no ticket

3. We shall make every effort to recover what we have _____.

   A. received   B. lost

4. The presents were concealed until Christmas morning so that everyone would _____.

    A. see them   B. be surprised

5. The sentinel _____.

    A. patrolled the entrances   B. called the meeting to order

6. Compared to other zoo animals, the _____ is gigantic.

    A. elephant   B. fox

7. My cousin's family visited us lately, about four _____ ago.

    A. years   B. weeks

8. We _____ the sign because it is quite conspicuous.

    A. nearly missed   B. easily noticed

9. Some fans taunted the umpires by _____.

    A. accusing them of poor eyesight   B. praising their fairness

10. A grave matter is _____.

    A. nothing to worry about   B. cause for alarm

Exercise 5.3: Definitions

Each expression below defines a word taught on pages 59–60. Enter that word in the space provided.

_____ **1.** get back again

_____ **2.** in a serious manner

_____ **3.** in the near past

_____ **4.** declare not to be true

_____ **5.** attracting attention

_____ **6.** greater in size than usual

_____ **7.** one who watches or guards

_____ **8.** righteous anger

_____ **9.** jeer at

_____ **10.** hide from sight

Exercise 5.4: Synonyms and Antonyms

Fill the blanks in column A with the required synonyms or antonyms, selecting them from column B.

	Column A	Column B
_____	1. synonym for *deny*	lately
_____	2. antonym for *conceal*	reproach
_____	3. synonym for *giant-like*	refuse
_____	4. antonym for *deny*	display
_____	5. synonym for *recover*	gigantic
_____	6. antonym for *conspicuous*	sentinel
_____	7. synonym for *taunt*	gravely
_____	8. synonym for *seriously*	concealed
_____	9. synonym for *recently*	confirm
_____	10. synonym for *sentry*	regain

HOMONYMS: *TWO, TOO, AND TO*

1. Use **two** when you mean the number "2."

   Crispus Attucks was six feet *two* inches.

2. Use **too** for the following:

   (a) when you mean "also."
   Attucks was shot dead, and Samuel Gray, *too*.

   (b) when you mean "excessively."
   It was *too* late.

3. Use **to** for the following:

   (a) as part of the infinitive form of a verb (*to* go, *to* eat, etc.).
   It was time *to* go.

   (b) as a preposition (a part of speech that combines with a noun or pronoun to form a phrase).
   I went *to* the store.
   Please give it *to* me.

Exercise 5.5: *Two, Too, To?*

1. Only _____ of us were left.

2. Don't you have anything _____ do?

3. This package is not _____ heavy.

4. Leave this matter _____ me.

5. I never saw _____ sisters more alike.

6. Mike is coming, and Sue, _____ .

7. Please step _____ the rear of the bus.

8. She spent eighty-_____ dollars.

9. Please listen _____ me.

10. I, _____ , want fair treatment.

LEARNING SOME ROOTS AND DERIVATIVES

Each word in bold type is a **root.** The words below it are its **derivatives.**

conceal *(v.)*	I will tell everything; I will *conceal* nothing.
concealment *(n.)*	Everything will be told. There will be no *concealment.*
conspicuous *(adj.)*	Some people wear *conspicuous* clothes.
conspicuously *(adv.)*	Some people dress *conspicuously.*
deny *(v.)*	We heard you *deny* the charges.
denial *(n.)*	We heard your *denial* of the charges.
grave *(adj.)*	The orange grove has suffered *grave* damage.
gravely *(adv.)*	Frost has *gravely* damaged the orange crop.
gravity *(n.)*	Oranges will be scarce because of the *gravity* of crop damage.
indignant *(adj.)*	The shoppers were *indignant* over the price increases.
indignantly *(adv.)*	The shoppers *indignantly* complained about the price increases.
indignation *(n.)*	The shoppers expressed their *indignation* over the price increases.

recover (v.)	It will be impossible to *recover* our losses.
recoverable *(adj.)*	Our losses are not *recoverable.*
recovery *(n.)*	*Recovery* of our losses is impossible.
taunt *(v.)*	Don't *taunt* her; she does not deserve it.
taunt *(n.)*	She does not deserve your *taunts*.

Exercise 5.6:   Roots and Derivatives

Fill each blank below with the root or derivative just listed that best completes the sentence.

1. Wouldn't you, too, be _____ if someone had opened your mail?

2. You say the housing shortage is not serious. I believe it is very _____.

3. The suspect's _____ of guilt did not convince the jury.

4. The police were praised for the quick _____ of the stolen gems.

5. I refused to hide the truth; I believed that _____ would be unwise.

6. At an emergency meeting, we discussed a matter of the utmost _____.

7. The NO SMOKING signs were _____ posted; everyone could see them.

8. I _____ refused to pay for the same thing twice.

9. Often, a lost opportunity is not _____.

10. You should not have called Mark "butterfingers" when he dropped the ball. It was a cruel _____.

Exercise 5.7:   Changing One Part of Speech to Another

1. Change the adjective *indignant* to a noun.   _____

2. Write a noun derived from the verb *recover*.   _____

3. Change the adjective *grave* to an adverb.   _____

4. Write an adjective derived from the verb *recover*.   _____

5. From what verb do we get the noun *denial*?   _____

6. Change the adjective *grave* to a noun.   _____

7. Write a noun derived from the verb *conceal*.   _____

8. Write the noun form of the verb *taunt*.   _____

9. Change the adjective *conspicuous* to an adverb.   _____

10. Change the adjective *indignant* to an adverb.   _____

IMPROVING YOUR SPELLING: ADDING PREFIXES

A **prefix** is a syllable added to the beginning of a word to form a new word. For example, the prefix *in-*, meaning "not," added to the beginning of *excusable*, forms the new word *inexcusable*, meaning "not excusable."

Learn these prefixes and their meanings:

Prefix	Meaning	Sample Word
dis-	not	*dis*courteous (not courteous)
in-	not	*in*human (not human)
mis-	wrongly	*mis*spelled (wrongly spelled)
pre-	beforehand	*pre*arranged (arranged beforehand)
re-	again	*re*write (write again)
un-	not	*un*necessary (not necessary)

Important: Do not omit or add a letter when attaching a prefix to a word. Keep **all** the letters of the prefix and **all** the letters of the word.

re + elect = reelect

mis + spell = misspell

un + necessary = unnecessary

dis + satisfied = dissatisfied

Exercise 5.8: Wordbuilding With Prefixes

Fill in the last two columns. Follow the sample below.

Prefix	Word	New Word	Meaning
un	+ necessary =	unnecessary	not necessary
1. dis-	+ passionate =		
2. in-	+ conspicuous =		
3. pre-	+ conceived =		
4. re-	+ apply =		
5. in-	+ conceivable =		
6. mis-	+ managed =		
7. un-	+ observable =		
8. pre-	+ heated =		

9. dis- + loyal   = _____   _____

10. re- + organizing = _____   _____

Exercise 5.9: Conciseness

Reduce each expression below to a single word beginning with a prefix. The first expression has been reduced as a sample.

1. not armed   = <u>**unarmed**</u>

2. joined again   = _____

3. not sanely   = _____

4. planned beforehand = _____

5. enact again   = _____

6. not necessarily   = _____

7. paid beforehand   = _____

8. not comfortable   = _____

9. filled again   = _____

10. wrongly understood = _____

IMPROVING YOUR COMPOSITION SKILLS: REPORTING AN INCIDENT

In the opening sentence of a report on an incident, it is important to answer such questions as **who? what? where? when? why?** and **how?** Note how Langston Hughes begins his report on the events of the night of March 5, 1770:

> **About nine o'clock that night, taunted by youngsters, a sentinel had knocked a boy down in front of the Custom House.**

The above sentence answers these questions:

WHEN? (About nine o'clock that night)

WHO? (a sentinel)

WHAT? (had knocked a boy down)

WHY? (taunted by youngsters)

WHERE? (in front of the Custom House)

Exercise 5.10: First Sentence of the Report on an Incident

Write the opening sentence of an incident that you saw, or heard, or read about. Make sure that your sentence answers at least four of the following questions: Who? What? Where? When? Why? How? Here is a further sample of what you are being asked to write:

> **Yesterday, at the Municipal Stadium, the Wildcats defeated the Pirates by a score of 7–6.**

Note that the above sample answers the following questions:

WHEN? (Yesterday)   WHERE? (Municipal Stadium)

WHO? (Wildcats)   WHAT? (defeated the Pirates)

HOW? (by a score of 7–6)

Now write your opening sentence on the lines below.

_____

_____

_____

_____

The Most Dangerous Game

by Richard Connell

Suppose that one dark night you were accidentally to fall into the sea from a speeding yacht and no one aboard had seen you fall. What would you do?

There was no sound in the night as Rainsford sat there but the muffled throb of the engine that drove the yacht swiftly through the darkness, and the swish and ripple of the wash of the propeller. Rainsford, reclining in a steamer chair, indolently puffed
5   on his favorite brier. "It's so dark," he thought, "that I could sleep without closing my eyes; the night would be my eyelids—"

An abrupt sound startled him. Off to the right he heard it, and his ears, expert in such matters, could not be mistaken. Again he heard the sound, and again. Somewhere, off in the blackness,
10   someone had fired a gun three times. Rainsford sprang up and moved quickly to the rail, mystified. He strained his eyes in the direction from which the reports had come, but it was like trying to see through a blanket. He leaped upon the rail and balanced himself there, to get greater elevation; his pipe, striking a rope,
15   was knocked from his mouth. He lunged for it; a short, hoarse cry came from his lips as he realized he had reached too far and had lost his balance. The cry was pinched off short as the blood-warm waters of the Caribbean Sea closed over his head.

He struggled up to the surface and tried to cry out, but the
20   wash from the speeding yacht slapped him in the face and the salt water in his open mouth made him gag and strangle. Desperately he struck out with strong strokes after the receding lights of the yacht, but he stopped before he had swum fifty feet. A certain coolheadedness had come to him; it was not the first time he had been
25   in a tight place. There was a chance that his cries could be heard

by someone aboard the yacht, but that chance was slender, and grew more slender as the yacht raced on. He wrestled himself out of his clothes, and shouted with all his power. The lights of the yacht became faint and ever-vanishing fireflies; then they were
30 blotted out entirely by the night.

Rainsford remembered the shots. They had come from the right, and doggedly he swam in that direction, swimming with slow, deliberate strokes, conserving his strength. For a seemingly endless time he fought the sea. He began to count his strokes; he
35 could do possibly a hundred more, he thought, and then—

Rainsford heard a sound. It came out of the darkness, a high, screaming sound, the sound of an animal in an extremity of anguish and terror.

UNDERSTANDING THE SELECTION

Exercise 6.1: Close Reading

In the blank space, write the *letter* of the choice that best completes the statement or answers the question.

1. The best description of conditions at the time of Rainsford's accident is _____ .

   (A) visibility poor, sea rough, water temperature cold
   (B) visibility zero, sea calm, water temperature warm
   (C) visibility fair, sea calm, water temperature cool

2. The word *brier,* as used in the second sentence of the selection, means a _____ .

   (A) musical instrument
   (B) tobacco pipe
   (C) hot drink

3. Which of the following actions by Rainsford was the result of panic? _____

   (A) swimming with strong strokes after the yacht
   (B) balancing himself on the rail
   (C) wrestling himself out of his clothes

4. Rainsford _____ .

   (A) did not have good eyesight
   (B) had had narrow escapes in the past
   (C) was not a good swimmer

5. In his struggle to reach safety, Rainsford was guided mainly by _____ .

   (A) the current
   (B) his knowledge of geography
   (C) his sense of hearing

6. The main cause of Rainsford's loss of balance was ____.

    (A) his eagerness to learn where the shots had come from
    (B) a swaying movement of the speeding yacht
    (C) his poor judgment

7. Which of the following lines do not contain a comparison? ____

    (A) lines 9–10
    (B) lines 11–13
    (C) lines 28–30

8. The sentence in lines 19–21 makes an appeal to every one of the reader's senses except the sense of ____.

    (A) touch
    (B) smell
    (C) taste

LEARNING NEW WORDS

Line	Word	Meaning	Typical Use
7	**abrupt** (adj.) ə-'brəpt	characterized by a sharp break; sudden; hasty; unexpected	Dale's *abrupt* departure took us by surprise; she did not even say goodbye.
		(*ant.* **leisurely**)	You'll never get there on time if you stick to your *leisurely* pace.
33	**conserve** (v.) kən-'sərv	protect from loss or being used up; preserve	To *conserve* electricity, turn off lights when they are not in use.
		(*ant.* **waste, squander**)	In a short time a spendthrift can *squander* a large sum of money.
33	**deliberate** (adj.) di-'lib-ə-rət	slow; not hurried; carefully thought out	Connie usually beats me in chess because she takes her time; she makes *deliberate* moves.
		(*ant.* **abrupt, impulsive, thoughtless**)	Roy's decision to drop out of the play was not *impulsive;* he had given it a great deal of thought.
32	**doggedly** (adv.) 'dȯg-əd-lē	stubbornly; obstinately; in an unshakable manner	Though the odds were against him, Tony fought *doggedly* to win.
14	**elevation** (n.) ˌel-ə-'vā-shən	height; altitude; height above sea level	In painting the ceiling, Charles had to use a ladder because the old chair didn't give him the necessary *elevation*.

29	**faint** *(adj.)* 'fānt	feeble; weak; barely perceptible	The witness replied in so *faint* a voice that it was difficult to hear what he was saying.
4	**indolently** *(adv.)* 'in-də-lənt-lē	lazily; idly	I spent the first day of my vacation *indolently,* not doing one bit of work.
		(ant. **industriously, busily**)	Everyone in the shop worked *industriously;* there was no sign of idleness.
22	**recede** *(v.)* ri-'sēd	go back; move back; withdraw	The flood victims could not return to their homes until the waters had *receded.*
		(ant. **advance**)	Prices on the stock exchange *advanced* to a new high.
27	**slender** *(adj.)* 'slen-dər	1. slight; small; meager	When we were behind by twelve points, our hopes of winning looked very *slender.*
		2. long and thin; not big around	A proper diet can help achieve and maintain a *slender* figure.
19	**surface** *(n.)* 'sər-fəs	the outside of anything; any face or side of a thing; top	For miles around the damaged tanker, the *surface* of the water was oily.

APPLYING WHAT YOU HAVE LEARNED

Exercise 6.2: Sentence Completion

Which of the two choices correctly completes the sentence? Write the *letter* of your answer in the space provided.

1. If you step on the brake _____, the vehicle will come to an abrupt halt.

    A. gradually   B. suddenly

2. _____ provide some extra elevation.

    A. High heels   B. Woolen gloves

3. You held on to the stick so doggedly that it was very _____ to take it away from you.

    A. easy   B. difficult

4. The faint ray from my flashlight was a sign that the batteries were _____.

    A. fresh   B. old

5. Everything seemed fine on the surface, but we had no way of telling what was _____ .

A. inside

B. outside

6. In a matter of importance, a deliberate decision is far better than _____ one.

A. an unhurried

B. a hasty

7. They worked indolently and accomplished _____ .

A. a great deal

B. very little

8. Please keep the outside door _____ ; we are trying to conserve heat.

A. closed

B. open

9. It is relaxing to watch the waves _____ and recede.

A. go back

B. advance

10. Camille's chances of being elected are slender, as _____ .

A. she is very popular

B. hardly anyone knows her

Exercise 6.3: Definitions

Each expression below defines a word taught on pages 70–71. Enter that word in the space provided.

_____ **1.** any face or side of a thing

_____ **2.** in a lazy manner

_____ **3.** height above sea level

_____ **4.** protect from being used up

_____ **5.** characterized by a sharp break

_____ **6.** move back

_____ **7.** in an unshakable manner

_____ **8.** not big around

_____ **9.** carefully thought out

_____ **10.** barely perceptible

Exercise 6.4: Synonyms and Antonyms

A. Replace each italicized word with a *synonym* from the vocabulary list on the next page.

_____ **1.** Do you become dizzy at a high *altitude*?

_____ **2.** The sun shone *feebly*.

_____ 3. This short belt is for someone with a *small* waist.

_____ 4. Why are you so *obstinately* opposed to our plan?

_____ 5. The *outside* of the apple was coated with jelly.

B. Replace each italicized word with an *antonym* from the vocabulary list.

_____ 6. Never did I have such *industrious* helpers.

_____ 7. The cold front *advanced*.

_____ 8. Are our resources being *wasted?*

_____ 9. He opened the door *deliberately*.

_____ 10. It was a *thoughtless* act.

Vocabulary List

conserved	deliberate
indolent	surface
elevation	receded
faintly	abruptly
doggedly	slender

LEARNING SOME ROOTS AND DERIVATIVES

Each word in bold type is a **root.** The words below it are its **derivatives.**

abrupt *(adj.)*	The meeting came to an *abrupt* end.
abruptly *(adv.)*	The meeting ended *abruptly*.
abruptness *(n.)*	The meeting ended with *abruptness*.
conserve *(v.)*	Steps are being taken to *conserve* our forests.
conservation *(n.)*	Steps are being taken for the *conservation* of our forests.
deliberate *(v.)*	I had to decide quickly. I had no chance to *deliberate*.
deliberate *(adj.)*	I had no time for *deliberate* consideration.
deliberately *(adv.)*	I could not consider the matter *deliberately*.
deliberation *(n.)*	There was no time for *deliberation*.

Note that "deliberate," when used as a verb, is pronounced di-'lib-ə-ˌrāt.

dogged *(adj.)*	My *dogged* opponent would not give in.
doggedly *(adv.)*	*Doggedly*, he continued to fight.
doggedness *(n.)*	He hoped to wear me down by his *doggedness*.

elevate (v.)	The firm is going to *elevate* my aunt to a higher post.
elevated (adj.)	She will hold the *elevated* position of vice-president.
elevation (n.)	A celebration is being planned in honor of her *elevation*.
faint (adj.)	Your flashlight emits a *faint* beam.
faintly (adv.)	Your flashlight shines *faintly*.
faintness (n.)	The *faintness* of the light shows that fresh batteries are needed.
indolent (adj.)	Last summer I was *indolent*.
indolently (adv.)	I spent my summer *indolently*.
indolence (n.)	I wasted my vacation in *indolence*.
recede (v.)	You can find interesting shells on the beach when the tide *recedes*.
recession (n.)	Interesting shells appear on the beach with the *recession* of the tide.
slender (adj.)	It is foolish to starve yourself to become *slender*.
slenderness (n.)	*Slenderness* is desirable, but not at the expense of health.
slenderize (v.)	To *slenderize*, you should exercise and follow a sane diet.
surface (n.)	The damage does not go below the *surface*.
superficial (adj.)	The damage is *superficial*.

Exercise 6.5: Roots and Derivatives

Fill each blank below with the root or derivative just listed that best completes the sentence.

1. The reducing salon claims it can _____ people who have put on too much weight.

2. What was left of the candle flickered _____ for a while and then went out altogether.

3. It is hard to tell whether we are going to have an advance in business activity or a(an) _____ .

4. You can't accuse Jim of _____ ; he has never been lazy.

5. The candidate mounted a(an) _____ platform to address the crowd.

6. Don't decide in a hurry. Take time to _____ .

7. Did the change occur gradually or _____ ?

8. When there is a lack of rainfall, _____ of water becomes absolutely necessary.

9. Her _____ in following up every clue enabled her to solve the puzzle.

10. The wound was _____ ; it did not extend below the surface of the skin.

Exercise 6.6: Similar or Related Words

Add a word similar in meaning to the other two. (*Hint:* See pages 73–74.) The first word has been added as a sample.

1. lazy; idle __**indolent**____

2. slowly; unhurriedly _____

3. obstinate; stubborn _____

4. haste; suddenness _____

5. raise; lift _____

6. idleness; laziness _____

7. preservation; protection _____

8. unexpectedly; hastily _____

9. retreat; withdrawal _____

10. weakness; feebleness _____

IMPROVING YOUR SPELLING: VERBS ENDING IN -*CEED*, -*CEDE*, AND -*SEDE*

1. Only three verbs end in -*ceed:*

   ex*ceed*   pro*ceed*   suc*ceed*

2. Other verbs with the above final sound end in -*cede:*

   re*cede*   *cede*   ac*cede*   pre*cede*
   se*cede*   con*cede*   inter*cede*

3. An exception is *supersede.* This is the only verb ending in -*sede.*

Exercise 6.7: -*CEED*, -*CEDE*, or -*SEDE*?

Complete the unfinished word.

1. Pro_____ to the nearest exit.
   (go ahead)

2. These instructions super_____ the old ones.
   (replace)

3. I am ready to inter_____ for you.
   (plead)

4. A parade will pre_____ the game.
   (come before)

5. Are you ready to con_____ defeat?
   (admit)

6. Who will suc_____ you?
   (come after)

7. Will prices re_____ from the recent highs?
   (move back)

8. Your spending should not ex_____ your earnings.
   (be more than)

9. Our team plans to se_____ from the league.
   (withdraw)

10. They will ac_____ to our proposal.
   (agree)

USING VERBS

Should you say, "I *swam*" or "I *swum?*" "The lock is *broken*" or "The lock is *broke?*" "Who *did* it?" or "Who *done* it?" To solve such problems, learn the principal parts of verbs.

Principal Parts of Verbs. A verb has three principal parts:

   1. The present tense (the part listed in the dictionary)

   2. The past tense

   3. The past participle

Regular verbs have the same spelling for the second and third principal parts—they simply add -*ed* to the present tense:

Present Tense	Past Tense	Past Participle
shout	shout*ed*	shout*ed*
conserve	conserv*ed*	conserv*ed*

Irregular verbs do not add -ed. They undergo either (1) a vowel change:

Present Tense	Past Tense	Past Participle
swim	swam	swum
come	came	come
drink	drank	drunk
lead	led	led
run	ran	run
spring	sprang	sprung
	(or sprung)	

or (2) a vowel change plus other changes:

break	broke	broken
do	did	done
freeze	froze	frozen
go	went	gone
ride	rode	ridden
tear	tore	torn

Two Important Suggestions:

1. Memorize the principal parts of irregular verbs. For example, *swim, swam, swum.*

2. After a helping verb *(is, are, was, were, have, has, had, has been,* etc.), use the third principal part, not the second. For example:

    The egg is *broken* (not *broke*).
    Has the lake *frozen* (not *froze*)?

Exercise 6.8: Supplying Principal Parts

Fill in the missing principal parts. Follow the sample given on the first line.

	Present Tense	Past Tense	Past Participle
1.	recede	receded	receded
2.	deny		
3.			done
4.		broke	
5.	dismay		
6.			ridden
7.		conceived	
8.	swim		
9.			gone
10.		squandered	

Exercise 6.9: Past Tense or Past Participle?

Complete the sentence.

1. He stopped before he had _____ fifty feet. (*swam* or *swum*)
2. The shots had _____ from the right. (*came* or *come*)
3. How many windows were _____? (*broke* or *broken*)
4. Who _____ that? (*done* or *did*)
5. She _____ most of the milk. (*drunk* or *drank*)
6. I should not have _____ it. (*torn* or *tore*)
7. A band _____ the parade. (*lead* or *led*)
8. By noon we had _____ seventy miles. (*rode* or *ridden*)
9. No one knew where they had _____. (*went* or *gone*)
10. Has the pond _____ yet? (*froze* or *frozen*)

IMPROVING YOUR COMPOSITION SKILLS: WORDS THAT APPEAL TO THE SENSES

To improve your skill in description, learn to use words that appeal to the reader's senses. Richard Connell offers a good example in lines 19–21:

> He struggled up to the surface and tried to cry out, but the wash from the speeding yacht slapped him in the face and the salt water in his open mouth made him gag and strangle.

Connell's sentence uses words that appeal to the followng senses:

HEARING: cry out, wash, slapped, gag, strangle
TASTE: salt water, mouth
TOUCH: slapped
SIGHT: speeding yacht

Exercise 6.10: Using Sense-Appeal Words

Write a brief description, appealing to at least two senses (the senses are sight, hearing, smell, taste, and touch). Write no more than three sentences.

Suggested Topics: Describe something that impressed you while you were in a bake shop, a burger shop, a pizza parlor, a fruit and vegetable store, or a florist's shop—or while you were at a game, or on a bus, or even at home. Here is a sample:

> **For breakfast I had a glass of orange juice, a bowl of hot oatmeal, some milk, a sliced ripe banana, and two pieces of crisp, buttered, golden-brown toast.**

Note that the sample uses these sense-appeal words:

TASTE: breakfast, orange juice, oatmeal, milk, ripe banana, buttered, toast
SIGHT: glass, orange, bowl, milk, ripe banana, buttered, golden-brown toast
TOUCH: hot
SMELL: orange juice, oatmeal, milk, banana, buttered, toast
HEARING: crisp

Here is another sample:

> **Going uphill, we passed a smoky tractor-trailer that was polluting the air with clouds of choking diesel fumes. But later, after we passed a highway mowing crew, the air was sweet with the perfume of freshly cut grass.**

Now write your description.

_____

_____

_____

_____

_____

_____

_____

The Overcoat

by Nikolay Gogol

The following selection is about a government clerk by the name of Akaky Akakyevitch Bashmatchkin. People made fun of him. Have you ever thought what it must be like to be teased by everyone?

No respect at all was shown him in the department. The porters, far from getting up from their seats when he came in, took no more notice of him than if a simple fly had flown across the vestibule. His superiors treated him with a sort of domineering chilliness. The head clerk's assistant used to throw papers under his nose without even saying: "Copy this" or "Here is an interesting, nice little case" or some agreeable remark of the sort, as is usually done in well-behaved offices. And he would take it, gazing only at the paper without looking to see who had put it there and whether he had the right to do so; he would take it and at once set to work to copy it. The young clerks jeered and made jokes at him to the best of their clerkly wit, and told before his face all sorts of stories of their own invention about him; they would say of his landlady, a woman of seventy, that she beat him, would enquire when the wedding was to take place, and would scatter bits of paper on his head, calling them snow. Akaky Akakyevitch never answered a word, however, but behaved as though there were no one there. It had no influence on his work even; in the midst of all this teasing, he never made a single mistake in his copying. Only when the jokes were too unbearable, when they jolted his arm and prevented him from going on with his work, he would bring out: "Leave me alone! Why do you insult me?" and there was something strange in the words and in the voice in which they were uttered. There was a note in it of something that aroused compas-

sion, so that one young man, new to the office, who, following the
example of the rest, had allowed himself to mock at him, suddenly
stopped as though cut to the heart, and from that time forth,
everything was, as it were, changed and appeared in a different
light to him. Some unnatural force seemed to thrust him away
from the companions with whom he had become acquainted,
accepting them as well-bred, polished people. And long afterwards, at moments of the greatest gaiety, the figure of the humble
little clerk with a bald patch on his head rose before him with his
heartrending words: "Leave me alone! Why do you insult me?"
and in those heartrending words he heard others: "I am your
brother." And the poor young man hid his face in his hands, and
many times afterwards in his life he shuddered, seeing how much
inhumanity there is in man, how much savage brutality lies
hidden under refined, cultured politeness, and, my God! even in a
man whom the world accepts as a gentleman and a man of honor.

UNDERSTANDING THE SELECTION

Exercise 7.1: Close Reading

In the blank space, write the *letter* of the choice that best completes the statement or
answers the question.

1. Akaky Akakyevitch was treated with disrespect by everyone except the _____.

    (A) porters
    (B) head clerk's assistant
    (C) young man new to the office

2. Akaky Akakyevitch _____.

    (A) never uttered a word of complaint
    (B) was engaged to marry his landlady
    (C) never made a mistake in copying

3. The young man new to the office _____.

    (A) could not appreciate harmless joking
    (B) felt that Akaky Akakyevitch was being cruelly treated
    (C) had no pity at all for Akaky Akakyevitch

4. The young man had joined in the teasing at first because _____.

    (A) his companions were doing it
    (B) Akaky Akakyevitch didn't mind
    (C) Akaky Akakyevitch had insulted him

5. When he heard the words "Leave me alone! Why do you insult me?" the young man _____.

    (A) was amused
    (B) realized that all men are brothers
    (C) realized that his companions were really cultured gentlemen

6. Who were Akaky Akakyevitch's worst tormentors? _____

    (A) the porters
    (B) the supervisors
    (C) the young clerks

7. The person or persons in charge of the office _____ the teasing of Akaky Akakyevitch.

    (A) tolerated
    (B) frowned upon but did not discourage
    (C) were not fully aware of

8. From the evidence in the selection, one may conclude that what happened to Akaky Akakyevitch was _____.

    (A) his own fault
    (B) just a sample of the widespread cruelty and inhumanity in human beings
    (C) most unlikely to happen to anyone else

LEARNING NEW WORDS

Line	Word	Meaning	Typical Use
7	**agreeable** (adj.) ə-'grē-ə-bəl	pleasing; pleasant; to one's taste or liking	Most people find that being with others is more *agreeable* than being alone.
		(ant. **disagreeable**)	The new lifeguard is very *disagreeable*; the old one was much more to our liking.
38	**brutality** (n.) brü-'tal-ət-ē	cruelty; savageness; inhumanity	The guard accused of *brutality* denied that he had ever beaten any prisoner.
24–5	**compassion** (n.) kəm-'pash-ən	sorrow or pity aroused by the suffering of another; sympathy; mercy	News of the earthquake aroused worldwide *compassion* and speeded relief to the sufferers.
35	**heartrending** (adj.) 'härt-ˌren-diŋ	causing intense grief; very distressing	The loss of a loved one is a *heartrending* experience.

32	**humble** *(adj.)* 'həm-bəl	1. low in rank or position; not important	Abe Lincoln rose from a *humble* laborer to the highest position in the land.
		(ant. **important***)*	
		2. not proud; modest; meek	If you are *humble* about your achievements, you will be better liked than if you boast about them.
		(ant. **proud***)*	
11	**jeer** *(v.)* 'jiər	speak or cry out in mockery, contempt, or scorn; mock; ridicule; scoff	When the outfielder dropped the ball, some of the fans rudely *jeered* him.
20	**jolt** *(v.)* 'jōlt	jar; shake up; interfere with roughly and abruptly	The occupants of the car were severely *jolted* when it was struck from behind by another vehicle.
4	**superior** *(n.)* sù-'pir-ē-ər	one who is above another in position or rank	The teacher's *superior* is the principal.
		(ant. **inferior***)*	Lisa has never beaten me in chess, but when it comes to tennis I am her *inferior*.
3–4	**vestibule** *(n.)* 'ves-tə-ˌbyül	lobby; passage or hall between the outer door and the inside of a building	I waited for you outside, but when it started to rain I stepped into the *vestibule*.
31	**well-bred** *(adj.)* 'wel-'bred	well brought up; refined; showing good manners; cultivated	George's rudeness and lack of consideration for others show that he is not a *well-bred* person.

APPLYING WHAT YOU HAVE LEARNED

Exercise 7.2: Sentence Completion

Which of the choices correctly completes the sentence? Write the *letter* of your answer in the space provided.

1. The manufacture of _____ fur garments does not involve brutality to animals.

    A. natural   B. artificial

2. _____ entering the interior of the building, you have to pass through the vestibule.

    A. Before   B. After

3. The sight of a _____ human being arouses my compassion.

    A. courteous   B. suffering

4. A _____ is the sergeant's superior.

    A. lieutenant   B. corporal

5. Mike, who is an excellent student, was jolted by his _____ mark in math.

    A. high   B. low

6. By its jeering, the audience clearly showed _____ for the speaker.

    A. disrespect   B. respect

7. Their _____ is a sign that they are well-bred.

    A. politeness   B. stubbornness

8. The scene in which the lovers are _____ is heartrending.

    A. married   B. separated

9. If the novel _____ you, select one that is more agreeable.

    A. pleases   B. displeases

10. The rank of _____ is not a humble one.

    A. private   B. colonel

Exercise 7.3: Definitions

Each expression below defines a word taught on pages 82–83. Enter that word in the space provided.

_____ **1.** pity aroused by another's suffering

_____ **2.** cry out in scorn

_____ **3.** causing intense grief

_____ **4.** showing good manners

_____ **5.** to one's liking

_____ **6.** one who is above another in rank

_____ **7.** shake up

_____ **8.** low in rank

_____ **9.** ruthless violence

_____ **10.** hall between outer door and inside of a building

Exercise 7.4: Synonyms and Antonyms

A. Replace each italicized word with a *synonym* from the vocabulary list below.

_____ **1.** Wait for me in the *lobby*.

_____ **2.** Have you no *sympathy?*

_____ **3.** Everyone was *jarred* by the explosion.

_____ **4.** Were the charges of *savageness* confirmed?

_____ **5.** At first they *mocked* us.

Vocabulary List

jolted	disagreeable
superior	heartrending
humble	jeered
well-bred	vestibule
compassion	brutality

B. Replace each italicized word with an *antonym* from the vocabulary list.

_____ **6.** Do you find shopping *pleasant?*

_____ **7.** The play ends with a *joyful* scene.

_____ **8.** You should not be so *proud*.

_____ **9.** Grandpa believes the new model cars are *inferior* to last year's.

_____ **10.** Your cousin's manners show that he is *uncultivated*.

LEARNING SOME ROOTS AND DERIVATIVES

Each word in bold type is a *root.* The words below it are its *derivatives.*

agree *(v.)* — They were willing to *agree.*

agreeable *(adj.)* — They were *agreeable.*

agreeably *(adv.)* — They received our suggestion *agreeably.*

brutal *(adj.)* — There was a *brutal* wrestling match on TV.

brutally *(adv.)* — The wrestlers fought *brutally.*

brutality *(n.)* — We objected to the *brutality* of the bout.

brutalize *(v.)* — Does wrestling *brutalize* people?

compassion (n.)	The nursing staff showed *compassion.*
compassionate (adj.)	They were *compassionate.*
compassionately (adv.)	They watched over their patients *compassionately.*

humble (adj.)	Why should you be so *humble?*
humble (v.)	Why should you *humble* yourself before others not half so good as you?
humbly (adv.)	Why should you act so *humbly?*
humility (n.)	Why should you show such *humility?*

jeer (v.)	It is rude to *jeer* the visiting team.
jeer (n.)	The visitors, however, paid little attention to these *jeers.*
jeeringly (adv.)	Still, a few girls shouted *jeeringly* at them.

| **jolt** (v.) | The jury's verdict *jolted* the defendant. |
| jolt (n.) | To the defendant, the jury's verdict was a severe *jolt.* |

superior (adj.)	Ralph is a *superior* chess player.
superior (n.)	In fact, he has yet to meet his *superior.*
superiority (n.)	His *superiority* in chess is obvious, for he has never been beaten.

Exercise 7.5: Roots and Derivatives

Fill each blank below with the root or derivative just listed that best completes the sentence.

1. The slender lad was no match for his husky opponent and would have been _____ beaten.

2. As _____ people, we feel pity for all who suffer.

3. Laura's defeat in the election shook her up badly; it was a severe _____ to her.

4. Managers earn more than cashiers because they hold _____ positions.

5. Friends should not exchange angry words just because they do not _____ on something unimportant.

6. One of my teammates _____ called me "the hitless wonder" after I had struck out for the sixth time.

7. You are too proud. You lack _____ .

8. No claim should be made that a product is better than others unless its _____ has clearly been proved.

9. Instead of being displeased, I was _____ surprised.

10. Some seniors are so proud that they will not _____ themselves by eating at the same table as sophomores and juniors.

Exercise 7.6: Defining Roots and Derivatives

Enter the word from pages 85–86 that matches the definition below.

_____ **1.** in a manner that shows sympathy

_____ **2.** cruel; inhuman; savage

_____ **3.** put into a low rank

_____ **4.** meekness; lack of pride

_____ **5.** in a pleasing way

_____ **6.** mocking remark; taunt

_____ **7.** modestly; in a manner that is not proud

_____ **8.** make savage

_____ **9.** full of sympathy; merciful

_____ **10.** result of jarring; shaking up

IMPROVING YOUR SPELLING: ADDING SUFFIXES TO ONE-SYLLABLE WORDS

The young man who had *jeered* at Akaky suddenly *stopped.*

In the above sentence, why is the *p* in *stop* doubled *(stopped)* when *-ed* is added, whereas the *r* in *jeer* is not doubled *(jeered)?* Here is the explanation:

1. **In a *one*-syllable word, like *stop*, that ends in *one* consonant preceded by *one* vowel,**

   we *double the final consonant before a suffix beginning with a vowel.*

WORD		SUFFIXES		NEW WORDS
stop	+	-ed, -ing, -age	=	stopped, stopping, stoppage
plan	+	-ed, -ing, -er	=	planned, planning, planner
hot	+	-er, -est	=	hotter, hottest
fun	+	-y	=	funny

   Note: y is often treated as a vowel.

2. If the final consonant comes after *two* vowels, as in *jeer*,

do *not* double the final consonant.

jeer	+	-ed, -ing	= jeered, jeering
fail	+	-ed, -ing	= failed, failing
greed	+	-y	= greedy

3. If the final consonant comes right after another consonant, as in *form*,

do *not* double the final consonant.

form	+	-ed, -ing	= formed, forming
cold	+	-er, -est	= colder, coldest
dust	+	-y	= dusty

TO DOUBLE OR NOT TO DOUBLE?

The following three questions and answers sum up the above three rules:

Question 1: Why do we double the **p** in **stop** when adding **ed?**

stop + ed = stopped

Answer: The **p** is a consonant preceded by one vowel in a one-syllable word.

Question 2: Why don't we double the **l** in **mail** when adding **ed?**

mail + ed = mailed

Answer: The **l** comes after two vowels.

Question 3: Why don't we double the **m** in **form** when adding **ed?**

form + ed = formed

Answer: The **m** comes after a consonant.

Exercise 7.7: Doubling or Not Doubling the Final Consonant

A. Write the new word.

Word	+	*Suffix*	=	*New Word*
1. step	+	-ing	=	_____
2. stoop	+	-ing	=	_____
3. dream	+	-er	=	_____
4. drum	+	-er	=	_____
5. stop	+	-age	=	_____
6. post	+	-age	=	_____
7. thick	+	-est	=	_____
8. thin	+	-est	=	_____

9. fog   +   -y   = _____

10. fish   +   -y   = _____

11. jolt   +   -ed   = _____

12. jar   +   -ed   = _____

13. swim   +   -er   = _____

14. firm   +   -er   = _____

15. slam   +   -ed   = _____

B. For each word at the left, complete the three derivatives indicated.

16. sin   _____ing   _____ed   _____er

17. warm _____ed   _____er   _____est

18. bag   _____ed   _____y   _____age

19. scoff _____ing   _____ed   _____er

20. show _____ing   _____ed   _____y

21. fat   _____er   _____est   _____y

22. leak _____ing   _____ed   _____age

23. tan   _____ed   _____er   _____est

24. mock _____ing   _____ed   _____er

25. lug   _____ing   _____ed   _____age

USING *THERE* AND *THEIR*

THERE

Use *there* if the very next word is a verb. Examples: *there is; there are; there used to be; there came,* etc.

> *There* is a broken egg in the box.

Use *there* when the meaning "in that place" is required.

> We lived *there.*

THEIR

Use *their* when the meaning "belonging to them" is required.

> They earned *their* pay.

1. The porters did not get up from _____ seats when Akaky came in.

2. He did not look to see who had put the paper _____.

3. The young clerks made fun of him to the best of _____ clerkly wit.

4. They told all sorts of stories of _____ own invention.

5. Pretend that _____ is no one _____.

6. _____ was something strange in his voice.

7. How much inhumanity _____ is in man!

8. He did not look to see who had put it _____.

9. Did you go _____?

10. The boys like _____ hamburgers well done.

IMPROVING YOUR COMPOSITION SKILLS: SUPPORTING A STATEMENT WITH INCIDENTS OR EXAMPLES

Nikolay Gogol begins his paragraph about Akaky Akakyevitch with the following statement:

> No respect at all was shown him in the department.

Having made that statement, Gogol has to back it up with supporting evidence, and that is exactly what he does. Immediately, in one sentence after another, he shows that the porters, the superiors, the head clerk's assistant, and the young clerks treated Akaky Akakyevitch with no respect at all.

Exercise 7.9: Using Incidents or Examples

Begin a paragraph with a statement. Then, as Gogol does, back up that statement with at least three incidents or examples.

If you wish, you may begin with one of the following statements:

1. No friendliness was shown us when we played on our rivals' home court.

2. Nothing went right on Friday.

3. Nobody that I spoke to was interested in joining our club.

4. Not a single one of the first half-dozen residents that I approached was willing to contribute to the Community Fund.

5. No one could tell me how to get to the Post Office.

Here is a sample of what you are asked to write:

> No one could tell me how to get to the Post Office. The first passerby I stopped said he was in a hurry and couldn't help me. A salesclerk in a video-rental shop told me she had never been to the Post Office. A shopper coming out of the supermarket advised me to inquire at a gas station, but the nearest one was a mile away.

Below, make your statement and support it with incidents or examples.

_____

_____

_____

_____

_____

_____

_____

_____

_____

Shane

by Jack Schaefer

Out of nowhere, a stranger rides into the small Western town where Bob lives. Bob's father gives the stranger a job, though he knows very little about him. Bob has always wanted to be like his father, but now something in the stranger makes Bob think of changing his mind.

Now I was not so sure. I wanted more and more to be like Shane, like the man I imagined he was in the past fenced off so securely. I had to imagine most of it. He would never speak of it, not in any way at all. Even his name remained mysterious. Just
5 Shane. Nothing else. We never knew whether that was his first name or last name or, indeed, any name that came from his family. "Call me Shane," he said, and that was all he ever said. But I conjured up all manner of adventures for him, not tied to any particular time or place, seeing him as a slim and dark and dashing
10 figure coolly passing through perils that would overcome a lesser man.

I would listen in what was closely akin to worship while my two men, father and Shane, argued long and amiably about the cattle business. They would wrangle over methods of feeding and
15 bringing steers up to top weight. But they were agreed that controlled breeding was better than open range running and that improvement of stock was needed even if that meant spending big money on imported bulls. And they would speculate about the chances of a railroad spur ever reaching the valley, so you could
20 ship direct without thinning good meat off your cattle driving them to market.

It was plain that Shane was beginning to enjoy living with us and working the place. Little by little the tension in him was

fading out. He was still alert and watchful, instinct with that
25 unfailing awareness of everything about him. I came to realize
that this was inherent in him, not learned or acquired, simply a
part of his natural being. But the sharp extra edge of conscious
alertness, almost of expectancy of some unknown trouble always
waiting, was wearing away.

30 Yet why was he sometimes so strange and stricken in his own
secret bitterness? Like the time I was playing with a gun Mr.
Grafton gave me, an old frontier model Colt with a cracked barrel
someone had turned in at the store.

He sat down on an upturned crate and beckoned me over.
35 "Your holster's too low. Don't let it drag full arm's length. Have
it just below the hip, so the grip is about halfway between your
wrist and elbow when the arm's hanging limp. You can take the
gun then as your hand's coming up and there's still room to clear
the holster without having to lift the gun too high."

40 "Gosh agorry! Is that the way the real gunfighters do?"
A queer light flickered in his eyes and was gone.

Line 24. *instinct:* filled

UNDERSTANDING THE SELECTION

Exercise 8.1: Close Reading
In the blank space, write the *letter* of the choice that best completes the statement or
answers the question.

1. Shane never talked about _____.

(A) guns
(B) the cattle business
(C) his past

2. When Shane first came to the ranch, he was very _____.

(A) sick
(B) tense
(C) relaxed

3. Bob's father _____.

(A) had to drive his cattle to market
(B) used to ship his cattle to market by rail
(C) could not agree with Shane about anything

4. Bob's pistol _____.

(A) had a cracked barrel
(B) had been bought from Mr. Grafton
(C) was too big for its holster

5. The selection suggests that Bob _____.

    (A) dislikes Shane
    (B) has a good imagination
    (C) does not hold a high opinion of his father

6. When the topic of conversation is _____, Shane does not react normally.

    (A) steers
    (B) railroads
    (C) gunfighters

7. The context in lines 25–27 reveals that _____.

    (A) **inherent** and **acquired** have similar meanings
    (B) **inherent** and **natural** have opposite meanings
    (C) **inherent** and **natural** have similar meanings

8. Who is the narrator? _____

    (A) Jack Schaefer
    (B) Bob
    (C) Shane

LEARNING NEW WORDS

Line	Word	Meaning	Typical Use
12	**akin** *(adj.)* ə-'kin	essentially similar or related; alike *(ant.* **different***)*	Running away from a problem is *akin* to cowardice.
24	**alert** *(adj.)* ə-'lərt	watchful and quick to meet danger; wide-awake *(ant.* **heedless***)*	The fire was reported early by an *alert* youngster who detected a faint odor of smoke. The *heedless* motorist left the car without removing the keys from the ignition.
13	**amiably** *(adv.)* 'ā-mē-ə-blē	good-naturedly; in a friendly way; pleasantly; agreeably	The principal turned down our request *amiably,* so that we remain on friendly terms.
8	**conjure (up)** *(v.)* 'kän-jər	cause to appear in a magic way; imagine; invent	Who is this mysterious friend you keep talking about? Is he a real person, or someone you have *conjured up?*

26	**inherent** *(adj.)* in-'hir-ənt	deeply infixed; intrinsic; belonging to or being a part of a person or thing by nature	Mr. Smith would make a good judge because of his *inherent* fairness.
37	**limp** *(adj.)* 'limp	not stiff or rigid; drooping; slack	As the air escaped, the balloon fell *limp*.
3	**securely** *(adv.)* si-'kyu̇ər-lē	safely; firmly; surely; in a safe manner (*ant.* **dangerously**)	Before mounting a ladder, check to see that it rests *securely* on a firm foundation.
18	**speculate** *(v.)* 'spek-yə-ˌlāt	guess; think about something in which evidence is too slight for certainty to be reached; reflect	Already the class is *speculating* about who our new teacher will be.
23	**tension** *(n.)* 'ten-shən	mental or emotional strain; inner unrest	With the score tied, the bases loaded, two out, and a count of two strikes on the batter, everyone in the ballpark was under severe *tension*.
14	**wrangle** *(v.)* 'raŋ-gəl	dispute noisily; argue; quarrel; bicker	Stop *wrangling*, you two! Can't you go through at least one day without an argument?

APPLYING WHAT YOU HAVE LEARNED

Exercise 8.2: Sentence Completion

Which of the two choices correctly completes the sentence? Write the *letter* of your answer in the space provided.

1. When I asked the salesgirl for help, she said amiably: _____ .

A. "I'll be with you in just a minute."   B. "Can't you see I'm busy?"

2. A _____ is expected to be especially alert.

A. passerby   B. sentinel

3. We have _____ neighbors; they are always wrangling.

A. quarrelsome   B. quiet

4. _____ I was under great tension.

   A. After learning I had passed,   B. The first time I acted in a play,

5. Sal's opinion is akin to mine; he believes we made a mistake and I _____.

   A. disagree   B. agree

6. The knot _____ because it had been securely tied.

   A. slipped open   B. held firm

7. Dad's shirts are _____ because he hates limp collars.

   A. starched   B. unstarched

8. I don't have to speculate about my birthday gift because I _____ I am getting a camera.

   A. hope   B. know

9. Paul's unselfishness is inherent; it is _____.

   A. intended to impress others   B. a part of his nature

10. Did people conjure up the flying saucers, or could they possibly have _____ them?

   A. seen   B. imagined

Exercise 8.3: Definitions

Each expression below defines a word taught on pages 94–95. Enter that word in the space provided.

_____ **1.** cause to appear in a magic way

_____ **2.** deeply infixed

_____ **3.** watchful and quick to meet danger

_____ **4.** dispute noisily

_____ **5.** not stiff or rigid

_____ **6.** essentially similar or related

_____ **7.** in a friendly way

_____ **8.** mental or emotional strain

_____ **9.** in a safe manner

_____ **10.** think about something in which evidence is too slight for certainty to be reached

Exercise 8.4: Synonyms and Antonyms

Fill the blanks in column A with the required synonyms or antonyms, selecting them from column B.

	Column A	Column B
_____	1. synonym for *guess*	tension
_____	2. antonym for *stiff*	akin
_____	3. synonym for *good-naturedly*	speculate
_____	4. synonym for *bicker*	securely
_____	5. antonym for *heedless*	amiably
_____	6. synonym for *strain*	inherent
_____	7. antonym for *different*	limp
_____	8. synonym for *imagine*	wrangle
_____	9. antonym for *dangerously*	alert
_____	10. synonym for *intrinsic*	conjure

LEARNING SOME ROOTS AND DERIVATIVES

Each word in bold type is a **root**. The words below it are its **derivatives**.

alert *(adj.)*	Tell everybody to be *alert.*
alert *(v.)*	*Alert* everyone to the danger.
alertly *(adv.)*	Tell everyone to proceed *alertly.*
alertness *(n.)*	Impress everyone with the need for *alertness.*
amiable *(adj.)*	She greeted us with an *amiable* smile.
amiably *(adv.)*	She welcomed us *amiably.*
amiability *(n.)*	She received us with *amiability.*
inherent *(adj.)*	The child has an *inherent* fondness for animals.
inherently *(adv.)*	The child is *inherently* fond of animals.
limp *(adj.)*	Notice that my arms are *limp.*
limply *(adv.)*	See how my arms hang *limply* at my sides.
limpness *(n.)*	Note the *limpness* of my arms.

secure *(adj.)*	Are your valuables *secure*?
secure *(v.)*	*Secure* your valuables by depositing them in a safe.
securely *(adv.)*	Have they been *securely* stored?
security *(n.)*	A safe provides *security*.
speculate *(v.)*	It is useless to *speculate* about the outcome.
speculation *(n.)*	*Speculation* about the outcome is a waste of time.
tense *(adj.)*	We were all *tense*.
tensely *(adv.)*	We waited *tensely*.
tension *(n.)*	Everyone was under *tension*.
wrangle *(v.)*	They *wrangled* over the date of delivery.
wrangle *(n.)*	The *wrangle* over the delivery date was finally settled.

Exercise 8.5: Roots and Derivatives

Fill each blank below with the root or derivative just listed that best completes the sentence.

1. Someone said there will be an early dismissal on Thursday, but unless it is confirmed we must regard it as _____.

2. Keep your valuables in a(n) _____ place.

3. The teacher complimented me on my _____ when I found an error on the board.

4. I was surprised at your cousin's _____; he used to be such a disagreeable fellow.

5. A flashing red light has been installed at the crossing to _____ people to approaching trains.

6. At his first skating lesson, my frightened brother _____ clung to my arm.

7. The art masterpiece was exhibited behind a transparent shield for reasons of

   _____.

8. At one point in the play, the suspense was so great that I became very _____.

9. Now that one dispute has been settled, we are becoming involved in another

   _____.

10. As there was no wind, the banner hung _____ by the flagpole.

Exercise 8.6: Defining Roots and Derivatives

Enter the word from pages 97–98 that matches the definition below.

_____	**1.** good-natured; agreeable
_____	**2.** noisy quarrel
_____	**3.** in a wide-awake manner
_____	**4.** warn; make watchful
_____	**5.** under mental or emotional strain; high-strung
_____	**6.** intrinsically
_____	**7.** slackness; lack of stiffness
_____	**8.** make safe; guard
_____	**9.** watchfulness in meeting danger
_____	**10.** agreeableness

IMPROVING YOUR SPELLING: FORMING CONTRACTIONS

My friend said: "You're not doing that quite right."

In the above sentence, _you're_ is a **contraction** (shortened form) of the words _you_ and _are:_

you + are = you're

Notice that an **apostrophe** takes the place of the missing letter _a_ in the word _are._

We commonly use contractions in conversations and friendly notes and letters.

Exercise 8.7: Separating Contractions

The first contraction has been separated as a sample.

1. we'll	=	__we__	__will__
2. you're	=	_____	_____
3. I've	=	_____	_____
4. it'll	=	_____	_____
5. he'd	=	_____	_____
6. I'll	=	_____	_____
7. they're	=	_____	_____
8. couldn't	=	_____	_____
9. we've	=	_____	_____
10. won't	=	_____	_____

Exercise 8.8: Writing Contractions

The first contraction has been written as a sample.

1. would not: **wouldn't** _____
2. there is: _____
3. let us: _____
4. has not: _____
5. it is: _____
6. he will: _____
7. were not: _____
8. must not: _____
9. you have: _____
10. we are: _____

11. she will: _____
12. was not: _____
13. we would: _____
14. here is: _____
15. they have: _____
16. do not: _____
17. who is: _____
18. I will: _____
19. have not: _____
20. will not: _____

USING PRONOUNS

A *pronoun* is a word used in place of a noun.

Bob said that *he* wanted to be like Shane.

In the above sentence, *he* is a pronoun because it is used in place of the noun *Bob*.

Just think how awkward it would be if we had to say:

Bob said that *Bob* wanted to be like Shane!

The pronoun *he* makes it unnecessary to repeat the noun *Bob*. Clearly, pronouns enable us to make language more pleasing.

Exercise 8.9: Nouns Replaced by Pronouns

In each sentence below, one pronoun has been printed in italics. What noun (or nouns) does that pronoun replace? Write the answer in the space provided.

SAMPLE: "Your holster's too low. Don't let *it* drag."

The pronoun *it* replaces the noun **holster.**

1. The customers should have been given all the facts. It was not right to mislead *them*.

   The pronoun *them* replaces the noun _____ .

2. When Dad asked for the newspaper, I gave it to *him*.

   The pronoun *him* replaces the noun _____ .

3. Peggy and Sue shouted: "Wait for *us!*"

   The pronoun *us* replaces the nouns _____.

4. I would listen as Father and Shane argued amiably. *They* would wrangle over methods of feeding and bringing steer up to top weight.

   The pronoun *They* replaces the nouns _____.

5. George thanked his classmates for *their* cheerful get-well cards.

   The pronoun *their* replaces the noun _____.

6. If I see your sister, I shall ask *her* to help.

   The pronoun *her* replaces the noun _____.

7. The fans chanted: "*We* want a touchdown!"

   The pronoun *We* replaces the noun _____.

8. I enjoyed the pie. *It* was delicious.

   The pronoun *It* replaces the noun _____.

9. When the nurse came in, *she* asked me for my name.

   The pronoun *she* replaces the noun _____.

10. "Sharks. Big *ones.*"

    The pronoun *ones* replaces the noun _____.

Exercise 8.10: Using Pronouns

Complete each statement below by inserting the required pronoun.

1. Bob and his father knew very little about Shane; _____ didn't even know his full name.

2. The book interested me so much that _____ couldn't put it down.

3. I looked for Judy, but I didn't see _____.

4. Please do not come up to the desk. Wait until _____ are called.

5. Pat can tell you where Nina and Isabel live. She has _____ addresses.

6. Keith takes music lessons; _____ is studying the guitar.

7. I'm sorry I disturbed you. Please excuse _____.

8. My cousins live in the South. I plan to visit _____ next summer.

9. Charlotte and I travel to school together, but _____ leave for home at different times.

10. We will gladly give you permission. All you have to do is to ask _____.

In discussing Shane, Jack Schaefer writes (line 4, page 92):

> **Even his name remained mysterious.** (Note that each of the next four sentences explains why the name was mysterious.) **Just Shane. Nothing else. We never knew whether that was his first name or last name or, indeed, any name that came from his family. "Call me Shane," he said, and that was all he ever said.**

Exercise 8.11: Using Reasons

Make a statement and in the next four sentences, as Schaefer did above, support that statement with reasons. Here is another sample of what you are asked to write:

> **Yesterday's weather was delightful. After some early morning cloudiness, there was bright sunshine for the rest of the day. The high was 78 at 3 in the afternoon, and the overnight low was 52. Gentle to moderate winds prevailed all day. The humidity was comfortably low.**

Here are some hints for a topic:

> Neighbors (Our neighbors are very cooperative—or uncooperative)
> Food (The meal was excellent—or poor)
> TV (The Academy Awards program was disappointing—or exciting)
> Sports (Our team's prospects are bright—or not too encouraging)
> Weather (On the weekend, the weather was miserable—or ideal)

Now make your statement and support it with four reasons.

_____

_____

_____

_____

_____

_____

_____

_____

_____

Review of Unit II

Review II.1: Vocabulary and Spelling

Fill in the missing letters of the *Word*. (Each space stands for one missing letter.) Then write the *Complete Word* in the blank space.

Definition	Word	Complete Word
1. not stiff	_ _ MP	_____
2. in a wide-awake manner	AL _ _ TLY	_____
3. righteously angry	_ _ _ _ GNANT	_____
4. lobby	VESTI _ _ _ _	_____
5. low in rank	_ _ MBLE	_____
6. go back	REC _ _ _	_____
7. good-natured	AM _ _ BLE	_____
8. able to be regained	RE _ _ _ _ RABLE	_____
9. causing intense anguish	_ _ _ RTRENDING	_____
10. mental or emotional strain	TEN _ _ _ _	_____
11. pleasing	AGR _ _ _ BLE	_____
12. in an unhurried way	_ _ _ _ BERATELY	_____
13. stubbornly	DOGG _ _ _ _	_____
14. pity for another's suffering	_ _ _ PASSION	_____
15. dealing only with the outside	SUPERFI _ _ AL	_____
16. protected from being used up	CONS _ _ _ _ D	_____
17. guessing	SPEC _ _ _ TING	_____
18. easily seen	_ _ _ SPICUOUS	_____
19. seriousness	GRA _ _ TY	_____
20. deeply infixed	INH _ _ _ NT	_____

Review II.2: Synonyms

To each line, add a word that has the *same meaning* as the first two words on the line. Choose your words from the vocabulary list.

Vocabulary List

 1. sentry; guard _____

 2. scoff; jeer _____

 3. alike; akin _____

 4. huge; giant-like _____

 5. lazily; indolently _____

 6. height; elevation _____

 7. invent; conjure up _____

 8. inhumanity; brutality _____

 9. unexpected; abrupt _____

10. firmly; securely _____

similar

idly

safely

imagine

savageness

gigantic

mock

sudden

sentinel

altitude

Review II.3: Antonyms

For each italicized word in column A, write the best *antonym* from column B.

Column A

Column B

_____ 1. *faint* resistance

_____ 2. very *agreeable* afternoon

_____ 3. *conserved* her savings

_____ 4. *elevation* of forty feet

_____ 5. *denied* the report

_____ 6. *alert* guard

_____ 7. *humble* with his superiors

_____ 8. *receding* prices

_____ 9. *akin* to mine

_____ 10. worked *indolently*

confirmed

depth

busily

unrelated

careless

strong

advancing

proud

unpleasant

squandered

Review II.4: Wordbuilding With Prefixes

Fill each blank with a word formed by adding one of the following prefixes to the word in parentheses.

IN-, UN-, DIS-, MIS-, PRE-

The first statement has been completed as a sample.

1. We met all of our expenses; not one bill remains __unpaid__. *(paid)*

2. Ralph was friendly at first, but he became _____. *(agreeable)*

3. We were not told the truth; we were _____. *(led)*

4. I tried to be _____ so that nobody would notice me. *(conspicuous)*

5. The damage is so slight that it is almost _____. *(observable)*

6. They had no protection; they felt _____. *(secure)*

7. I expected the book to be dull, but I soon found that my _____ opinion was wrong. *(conceived)*

8. The sentries usually carry weapons, but that night they were _____. *(armed)*

9. Jack is calm and _____. *(passionate)*

10. Mother was alarmed, but Dad was _____. *(dismayed)*

Review II.5: Sentence Completion

Complete each sentence below with the most appropriate word from the following vocabulary list:

Vocabulary List

conjured	surface	jolted
concealed	lately	receded
inherent	securely	doggedly
slender	wrangled	jeered

1. It took us a long time to reach an agreement; we _____ for hours.

2. The sign may be blown away if it is not fastened _____.

3. All the facts have been disclosed. Nothing has been _____.

4. If the trouble is on the _____, it is easy to detect.

5. Anyone can be _____ by bad news if it comes suddenly.

6. Is this an excuse you have _____ up, or did it really happen?

7. The suspect was asked several questions, but he _____ remained silent.

8. I haven't seen you for the past two weeks. Where have you been spending your time _____?

9. Amy is very _____; this belt is too long for her.

10. When the results were announced, some of the disappointed fans _____ the decision.

Review II.6: Roots and Derivatives

On lines B and C, write the required forms of the italicized word on line A.

1. A. She spoke *tensely.*

   B. She spoke with _____ in her voice.

   C. She was _____ when she spoke.

2. A. People want *security.*

   B. People want to live _____ .

   C. People want to be _____ .

3. A. We made an *indignant* protest.

   B. We protested _____ .

   C. We protested with _____ .

4. A. A bullfight is usually *brutal.*

   B. A bullfight usually involves _____ .

   C. A bullfight usually ends _____ .

5. A. He tried to enter *inconspicuously.*

   B. He tried to enter in an _____ manner.

   C. He tried to enter without being _____ .

6. A. Abe Lincoln conducted himself with *humility.*

   B. Abe Lincoln was a _____ man.

   C. Abe Lincoln conducted himself _____ .

7. A. I was too *indolent* to get up early.

   B. _____ kept me from getting up early.

   C. Instead of getting up early, I remained _____ in bed.

8. A. Do you have *compassion* for the unfortunate?

   B. Are you _____ toward the unfortunate?

   C. Do you regard the unfortunate _____ ?

9. A. *Denying* the obvious truth is senseless.

   B. To _____ the obvious truth is senseless.

   C. _____ of the obvious truth is senseless.

10. A. They departed *abruptly.*

    B. They made an _____ departure.

    C. They left with _____ .

11. A. You were *amiable* to the visitors.

    B. You showed _____ to the visitors.

    C. You behaved _____ toward the visitors.

12. A. Some garments have *slenderizing* lines.

   B. Some garments are designed to make you look _____.

   C. Some garments give the wearer the appearance of _____.

13. A. Don't rush. Proceed at a *deliberate* pace.

   B. Don't rush. Proceed with _____.

   C. Don't rush. Proceed _____.

14. A. Robert Fulton *doggedly* pursued his goal.

   B. Robert Fulton pursued his goal with _____ determination.

   C. Robert Fulton showed _____ in pursuing his goal.

15. A. For me it was a *disagreeable* surprise.

   B. I was _____ surprised.

   C. It was not an _____ surprise for me.

16. A. Did you spend all your time in *idleness?*

   B. Did you stand _____ by all the time?

   C. Were you _____ all the time?

17. A. Can we *recover* our deposit?

   B. Is there a chance for the _____ of our deposit?

   C. Is our deposit _____?

18. A. Drive *alertly* to prevent accidents.

   B. _____ behind the wheel prevents accidents.

   C. An _____ driver prevents accidents.

19. A. Pollution is a very *grave* problem.

   B. Pollution is a problem that must be _____ considered.

   C. Pollution is a problem of the utmost _____.

20. A. The *faintness* of the witness's voice made it difficult to hear her.

   B. The witness spoke so _____ that she could scarcely be heard.

   C. Because of her _____ voice, it was difficult to hear the witness.

Review II.7: Concise Writing

In the space provided, rewrite the following paragraph to make it more concise. (*Hint:* Reduce each boldfaced expression to a single word.) The opening sentence will be rewritten to help you get started.

> The experience was **not to our liking.** Of course, we had not expected to be treated **in a friendly way.** As we entered the **hallway between the outside door and the inside of the building,** we were greeted by numerous **easily visible** signs proclaiming "Beat Benson!" Our chief tormentors were not our opponents on the court but the **students who were watching from the stands.** They missed no chance to **jeer at** us **in a mocking way,** especially when we made errors, but they did not **cause us to lose courage.** In spite of the **emotional strain,** we proceeded **in an unshakable manner** to do what we had come to do. We won the game.

The experience was disagreeable. _____

_____

_____

_____

_____

_____

_____

_____

_____

_____

_____

_____

_____

_____

My Name Is Aram

by William Saroyan

Suppose your teacher were to blame you for something that another pupil has done. You insist that you are innocent, but she does not believe you. Would you tell her who the guilty person is? Why?

My cousin Arak was a year and a half younger than me, round-faced, dark, and exceptionally elegant in manners. It was no pretense with him. His manners were just naturally that way, just as my manners were bad from the beginning. Where Arak would
5 get around any sort of complication at school with a bland smile that showed his front upper teeth, separated, and melted the heart of stone of our teacher, Miss Daffney, I would go to the core of the complication and with noise and vigor prove that Miss Daffney or somebody else was the culprit, not me, and if need be, I would
10 carry the case to the Supreme Court and prove my innocence.

I usually got sent to the office. In some cases I would get a strapping for debating the case in the office against Mr. Derringer, our principal, who was no earthly good at debates. The minute I got him cornered he got out his strap.

15 Arak was different; he didn't care to fight for justice. He wasn't anywhere near as bright as me, but even though he was a year and a half younger than me, he was in the same grade. I usually won all my arguments with my teachers, but instead of being glad to get rid of me they refused to promote me, in the hope, I believe,
20 of winning the following semester's arguments and getting even. That's how it happened that I came to be the oldest pupil in the fifth grade.

One day Miss Daffney tried to tell the world I was the author of the poem on the blackboard that said she was in love with Mr.

25 Derringer, and ugly. The author of the poem was my cousin Arak, not me. Any poem I wrote wouldn't be about Miss Daffney, it would be about something worthwhile. Nevertheless, without mentioning any names, but with a ruler in her hand, Miss Daffney stood beside my desk and said, I am going to find out who is
30 responsible for this horrible outrage on the blackboard and see that he is properly punished.

He? I said. How do you know it's a boy and not a girl?

Miss Daffney whacked me on the knuckles of my right hand.

I jumped out of my seat and said, You can't go around whacking
35 me on the knuckles. I'll report this.

Sit down, Miss Daffney said.

I did. She had me by the right ear, which was getting out of shape from being grabbed hold of by Miss Daffney and other teachers.

UNDERSTANDING THE SELECTION

Exercise 9.1: Close Reading

In the blank space, write the *letter* of the choice that best completes the statement.

1. The narrator states that he is _____.

   (A) younger than his cousin
   (B) in the habit of arguing with teachers
   (C) the author of the poem on the blackboard

2. Arak is able to escape punishment _____.

   (A) with the help of his smile and good manners
   (B) by never doing anything wrong
   (C) because he is too young to be punished

3. The narrator has been in trouble with _____.

   (A) Miss Daffney only
   (B) Miss Daffney, Mr. Derringer, and other teachers
   (C) Miss Daffney and Mr. Derringer

4. In comparison with Arak, the narrator claims to be much _____.

   (A) less bright
   (B) more polite
   (C) brighter

5. The selection proves _____.

   (A) that Miss Daffney is in love
   (B) neither that Miss Daffney is in love, nor that she is ugly
   (C) that Miss Daffney is not ugly

6. It would be INCORRECT to say that Miss Daffney had a class of ＿＿＿ .

    (A) fifth graders
    (B) fifth-grade boys
    (C) fifth-grade boys and girls

7. The narrator ＿＿＿ .

    (A) does not consider himself superior to teachers
    (B) refuses to admit that there is anything wrong with him
    (C) admits that he did not win all of his arguments with teachers

8. The narrator's claim that ＿＿＿ is disproved by the selection.

    (A) Miss Daffney has a heart of stone
    (B) Arak is a year and a half younger
    (C) Mr. Derringer is no earthly good at debates

LEARNING NEW WORDS

Line	Word	Meaning	Typical Use
5	**bland** *(adj.)* 'bland	gentle; mild; smooth and soothing	Seeing that I was upset, my sister spoke to me in *bland* tones so as not to irritate me further.
		(ant. **irritating***)*	Dr. Harris suggested a milder shampoo to Mother because the one she was using was too *irritating* for her skin.
5	**complication** *(n.)* ˌkäm-plə-'kā-shən	difficult state of affairs; difficulty; confused situation	Those who spend more than they earn often get into the *complication* of having to make new loans to pay off old ones.
7	**core** *(n.)* 'kōr	central, basic, inmost part; heart; center	The *core* of an apple is the part that contains the seeds.
9	**culprit** *(n.)* 'kəl-prit	person guilty of a fault or crime; offender	I was surprised to learn that you were to blame because I had thought all along that Jerry was the *culprit*.
2	**elegant** *(adj.)* 'el-i-gənt	very refined; showing good taste; correct and polished; excellent	The *elegant* manner in which my aunt furnished her apartment shows that she has good taste.

| | | (*ant.* **crude**) | | In the comic strip there were *crude* spellings, such as "sez" (*says*), "wuz" (*was*), and "luv" (*love*). |

2	**exceptionally** (*adv.*) ik-'sep-shən-əl-ē	in an out-of-the-ordinary way; unusually; uncommonly		A genius is a person of *exceptionally* high intelligence.
30	**outrage** (*n.*) 'aut-ˌrāj	act of violence showing no regard for others; offense; insult		Anyone who willfully destroys public property is committing an *outrage* against all of us.
2–3	**pretense** (*n.*) 'prē-ˌtens	make-believe; false show; pretext		Was Bruce's bandaged arm a *pretense* to avoid work, or a real injury?
20	**semester** (*n.*) sə-'mes-tər	half of a school year; term		In our school the first *semester* begins in September and ends in January.
8	**vigor** (*n.*) 'vig-ər	energy; force; power; active strength		Dad joined in our game without his usual *vigor;* he had had a hard day on the job.

APPLYING WHAT YOU HAVE LEARNED

Exercise 9.2: Sentence Completion

Which of the two choices correctly completes the sentence? Write the *letter* of your answer in the space provided.

1. Why did you _____ her? She is not the culprit.

   A. trust   B. blame

2. In most schools the second semester ends in _____.

   A. June   B. February

3. My little brother made a pretense of being asleep; in reality he was _____.

   A. fast asleep   B. listening to our conversation

4. When Phyllis _____, her physician ordered her on a bland diet.

   A. had an irritated stomach   B. was twenty pounds underweight

5. Wouldn't you consider the _____ of a hospital an outrage?

    A. surroundings   B. bombing

6. Eating steak with _____ is not an example of elegant table manners.

    A. your fingers   B. knife and fork

7. I finished in 30 minutes, which was exceptionally low because _____.

    A. half of my classmates took 30 minutes   B. none of my classmates took less than 40 minutes

8. By the eleventh round there was no vigor behind the champion's punches; he seemed to have used up all his _____.

    A. tricks   B. energy

9. Our discussion so far has dealt with the _____ of the problem. I hope we will now get to the core of the matter.

    A. heart   B. surface

10. Chuck gets into frequent complications because he _____.

    A. is often mistaken for his twin brother   B. never falls behind in any subject

Exercise 9.3: Definitions

Each expression below defines a word taught on pages 111–112. Enter that word in the space provided.

_____ **1.** in an out-of-the-ordinary way

_____ **2.** act of violence showing no regard for others

_____ **3.** smooth and soothing

_____ **4.** active strength

_____ **5.** central, basic, inmost part

_____ **6.** false show

_____ **7.** difficult state of affairs

_____ **8.** correct and polished

_____ **9.** half of a school year

_____ **10.** person guilty of a fault or crime

Exercise 9.4: Synonyms and Antonyms

Fill the blanks in column A with the required synonyms or antonyms, selecting them from column B.

Column A		Column B
_____	1. synonym for *insult*	semester
_____	2. synonym for *pretext*	complication
_____	3. synonym for *energy*	core
_____	4. synonym for *unusually*	vigor
_____	5. synonym for *center*	culprit
_____	6. antonym for *irritating*	exceptionally
_____	7. synonym for *term*	elegant
_____	8. antonym for *crude*	pretense
_____	9. synonym for *offender*	bland
_____	10. synonym for *difficulty*	outrage

LEARNING SOME ROOTS AND DERIVATIVES

Each word in bold type is a **root.** The words below it are its **derivatives.**

bland *(adj.)* This is a *bland* shampoo.

blandly *(adv.)* It *blandly* cleanses the hair and scalp.

blandness *(n.)* Because of its *blandness*, it can safely be used by persons with sensitive skin.

complicate *(v.)* The star of the show would *complicate* our problems if she were to get laryngitis.

complicated *(adj.)* Such an unlucky development would put us into a *complicated* situation.

complication *(n.)* Only if we had a capable understudy could we get out of such a *complication.*

elegant *(adj.)* Linda has *elegant* taste.

elegantly *(adv.)* She dresses *elegantly.*

elegance *(n.)* She shows *elegance* in her choice of clothes.

exception *(n.)* The others did poorly, with the *exception* of Karen.

exceptional *(adj.)* She has an *exceptional* mind.

exceptionally *(adv.)*	She is *exceptionally* bright.
outrage *(n.)*	The pollution of our rivers is an *outrage*.
outrage *(v.)*	Continued pollution of our rivers is sure to *outrage* public opinion.
outrageous *(adj.)*	The pollution of our rivers is *outrageous*.
outrageously *(adv.)*	Our rivers have been *outrageously* polluted.
pretend *(v.)*	Don't *pretend*.
pretense *(n.)*	Don't make *pretenses*.
pretender *(n.)*	Don't be a *pretender*.
vigor *(n.)*	Sam did not have his usual *vigor*.
vigorous *(adj.)*	He was not so *vigorous* as usual.
vigorously *(adv.)*	He walked less *vigorously* than usual.
invigorate *(v.)*	He needs a good rest; it will *invigorate* him.

Exercise 9.5: Roots and Derivatives

Fill each blank below with the root or derivative just listed that best completes the sentence.

1. If he calls you names again, don't answer him. Just _____ you haven't heard.

2. There was nothing _____ about the cake. It was just an ordinary birthday cake.

3. The clean mountain air will _____ you and make you feel strong and energetic.

4. Last week's math problems were not too difficult, but the ones we are doing now are more _____ .

5. Some of the waiters were very refined, but ours had no _____ at all.

6. It will be easier to settle the problem if you are not around; your presence will only _____ matters.

7. The description on the label says that this is "a gentle and soothing ointment of exceptional _____ ."

8. Cathy has good taste in clothes; she is always _____ dressed.

9. When attacked, the small nation fought back _____ , with all the force and power at its command.

10. I am insulted and offended by what you said. It is a(n) _____ lie.

Exercise 9.6: Similar or Related Words

Add a word similar in meaning to the other words or expressions. (*Hint:* See pages 114–115.) The first word has been added as a sample.

1. mildly; gently ___**blandly**___

2. powerful; forceful _____

3. unusual instance; case that does not follow the rule _____

4. in a very refined way; excellently _____

5. insultingly; in an offensive manner _____

6. person who makes believe; one who puts on a false show _____

7. give life and energy to; strengthen _____

8. offend; insult _____

9. unusual; uncommon _____

10. confuse; make difficult _____

IMPROVING YOUR SPELLING: WORDS ENDING IN -ABLE AND -IBLE

A. You can tell that an adjective ends in *-able* (rather than *-ible*), if you can trace it to a noun ending in *-ation*. For example:

commend*ATION*	commend*ABLE*
imagin*ATION*	imagin*ABLE*
irrit*ATION*	irrit*ABLE*

Exception: sens*ation*—sens*ible*

B. Apart from the above clue, there is no easy way to tell whether an adjective ends in *-able* or *-ible*. You will have to learn each word separately and consult the dictionary when in doubt. Study the following:

-ABLE Adjectives		*-IBLE Adjectives*	
agreeable	desirable	defensible	reducible
amiable	excusable	divisible	responsible
believable	favorable	horrible	reversible
conceivable	probable	permissible	terrible
dependable	usable	possible	visible

C. Note that the suffix *-able* or *-ible* does NOT change when a prefix is added:

dis	+ agree*able*	= disagree*able*
in	+ divis*ible*	= indivis*ible*
im	+ prob*able*	= improb*able*
ir	+ respons*ible*	= irrespons*ible*

Exercise 9.7: *-ABLE* or *-IBLE?*

1. horr_____
2. inconceiv_____
3. disagree_____
4. imposs_____
5. unimagin_____

6. irrespons_____
7. us_____
8. sens_____
9. commend_____
10. invis_____

11. The forecast says rain is prob_____ tomorrow.

12. The weather will be unfavor_____ .

13. ". . . one nation, under God, indivis_____, with liberty and justice for all."

14. You got 100% on that test? It's unbeliev_____!

15. Is crossing out permiss_____?

16. By the time we arrived, all the desir_____ seats had been taken.

17. You can wear this jacket on both sides; it's revers_____ .

18. The fraction 6/8 is reduc_____ to 3/4.

19. Don't try to make up excuses for what you did. Your behavior was indefens_____ .

20. I wouldn't use that old ladder if I were you. It's undepend_____ .

USING PRONOUNS AS SUBJECTS AND OBJECTS

Aram is an excellent storyteller, despite his repeated misuse of the pronoun *me:*

"My cousin Arak was a year and a half younger than *me . . .*"
"He wasn't anywhere near as bright as *me . . .*"

If the author had wanted Aram to use standard English, he would have had him say *I*, not *me*, in the above sentences.

Note the proper use of *I:*

QUESTION: My cousin was younger than _____ (*I* or *me*).

ANSWER: My cousin was younger than *I*.

EXPLANATION: *I* is correct because it is the subject of the understood verb *was:* "My cousin was younger than *I (was).*" It is incorrect to say "My cousin was younger than *me (was).*"

HINT: In a sentence like the above, always picture in your mind the understood verb (for example, *was*). It will help you choose the correct answer.

Note the proper use of *me:*

QUESTION: The class elected Jill and _____ (*I* or *me*).

HINT: In a case like the above, construct two sentences in your mind. Then combine them for the correct answer, as follows:

Sentence 1: The class elected Jill.

Sentence 2: The class elected *me* (not *I*).

Answer: The class elected Jill and *me.*

EXPLANATION: *Me* (together with *Jill*) is the object of the verb *elected.*

Note what happens when we turn the above sentence around:

QUESTION: Jill and _____ (*I* or *me*) were elected by the class.

HINT: Again, construct two sentences in your mind. Then combine them, as follows:

Sentence 1: Jill was elected by the class.

Sentence 2: *I* (not *me*) was elected by the class.

Answer: Jill and *I* were elected by the class.

EXPLANATION: *I* (together with *Jill*) is the subject of the verb *were elected.*

From the above examples we can see that the *I* form of the pronoun is for use as a subject, and the *me* form is for use as an object. Other pronouns, too, may have one form for a subject and another for an object. Learn the following:

Column A	**Column B**
For Use as a Subject	*For Use as an Object*
(known as **Nominative Case**)	(known as **Objective Case**)
I	me
you	you
he	him
she	her
it	it
we	us
they	them

Note that the pronouns *you* and *it* can be used both as subject and object. Also, the pronoun *I* is always capitalized; the other pronouns are capitalized when they begin a sentence.

Exercise 9.8: Using the Right Pronoun
Complete the sentence.

1. Mother called my sister and _____ *(I, me).*
2. Eileen is a year and a half older than _____ *(I, me).*
3. George is not nearly so amiable as _____ *(he, him).*
4. They probably know more math than _____ *(we, us).*
5. Paula and _____ *(she, her)* have always been friends.
6. No players have done more for the team than _____ *(they, them).*
7. Fred and _____ *(he, him)* are the only ones who have bought tickets.
8. We will meet you and _____ *(they, them)* at the clubhouse.
9. Do you know that Anne and _____ *(I, me)* are cousins?
10. You and _____ *(we, us)* have never been able to agree.

IMPROVING YOUR COMPOSITION SKILLS: MAKING A COMPARISON

If we analyze William Saroyan's first paragraph on page 109, we can see the following:

First Three Sentences

Saroyan compares Arak's manners and those of the narrator. Arak's are "exceptionally elegant." The narrator's are "bad."

Rest of the Paragraph

Saroyan gives an example of what happens when the boys get into trouble. "Elegant" manners enable Arak to escape punishment. "Bad" manners get the narrator into deeper trouble.

Exercise 9.9: Comparing Two Persons

Write a paragraph comparing two persons. First, identify the persons (do not use real names) and explain one way in which they differ. In the rest of the paragraph, give an example of how that difference produces different outcomes for the two persons.

Hints for Topics

Compare yourself with another person, or compare two persons with each other. If you wish, you may compare two things, two places, or two animals.

Sample Paragraph

My sister Doreen is exceptionally careful, but I am inclined to be careless. Before she leaves in the morning, she checks her room and makes sure she has taken with her everything she will need. I, on the other hand, may forget to turn off the lights, or to take my lunch, and there have even been times when I couldn't get into the house because I had forgotten to take my key.

Below, write your paragraph.

_____

_____

_____

_____

_____

_____

_____

_____

_____

_____

_____

_____

_____

_____

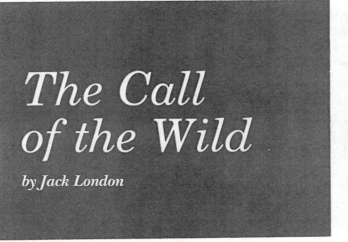

The Call of the Wild

by Jack London

As soon as gold is discovered in Alaska, there is a demand for powerful dogs capable of service in the frozen North. Buck, a huge and intelligent dog, is kidnapped from his sunny California home and shipped north by rail and wagon. The following is what happens to him after he has been a prisoner for forty-eight hours.

Four men gingerly carried the crate from the wagon into a small, high-walled back yard. A stout man, with a red sweater that sagged generously at the neck, came out and signed the book for the driver. That was the man, Buck divined, the next tormentor,
5 and he hurled himself savagely against the bars. The man smiled grimly, and brought a hatchet and a club.

"You ain't going to take him out now?" the driver asked.

"Sure," the man replied, driving the hatchet into the crate for a pry.

10 There was an instantaneous scattering of the four men who had carried it in, and from safe perches on top the wall they prepared to watch the performance.

Buck rushed at the splintering wood, sinking his teeth into it, surging and wrestling with it. Wherever the hatchet fell on the
15 outside, he was there on the inside, snarling and growling, as furiously anxious to get out as the man in the red sweater was calmly intent on getting him out.

"Now, you red-eyed devil," he said, when he had made an opening sufficient for the passage of Buck's body. At the same time
20 he dropped the hatchet and shifted the club to his right hand.

And Buck was truly a red-eyed devil, as he drew himself together for the spring, hair bristling, mouth foaming, a mad glitter in his blood-shot eyes. Straight at the man he launched his one hundred and forty pounds of fury, surcharged with the pent
25 passion of two days and nights. In mid air, just as his jaws were about to close on the man, he received a shock that checked his body and brought his teeth together with an agonizing clip. He whirled over, fetching the ground on his back and side. He had never been struck by a club in his life, and did not understand.
30 With a snarl that was part bark and more scream he was again on his feet and launched into the air. And again the shock came and he was brought crushingly to the ground. This time he was aware that it was the club, but his madness knew no caution. A dozen times he charged, and as often the club broke the charge
35 and smashed him down.

After a particularly fierce blow he crawled to his feet, too dazed to rush. He staggered limply about, the blood flowing from nose and mouth and ears, his beautiful coat sprayed and flecked with bloody slaver. Then the man advanced and deliberately dealt him
40 a frightful blow on the nose. All the pain he had endured was as nothing compared with the exquisite agony of this. With a roar that was almost lionlike in its ferocity, he again hurled himself at the man. But the man, shifting the club from right to left, coolly caught him by the under jaw, at the same time wrenching down-
45 ward and backward. Buck described a complete circle in the air, and half of another, then crashed to the ground on his head and chest.

For the last time he rushed. The man struck the shrewd blow he had purposely withheld for so long, and Buck crumpled up and
50 went down, knocked utterly senseless.

Line 4. *divined:* guessed

Line 17. *intent:* determined

Line 24. *pent:* shut up

Line 41. *exquisite:* acute

UNDERSTANDING THE SELECTION

Exercise 10.1: Close Reading

In the blank space, write the *letter* of the choice that best completes the statement.

1. When they hear that Buck is about to be removed from the crate, the four delivery men _____ .

   (A) do not stay to see what will happen
   (B) are thoroughly frightened
   (C) show no fear

2. The blow that causes Buck the most pain is the one delivered to his _____.

   (A) under jaw
   (B) nose
   (C) head

3. At no time in the furious struggle does Buck _____.

   (A) completely lose consciousness
   (B) throw the man in the red sweater off balance
   (C) know with what he has been hit

4. The selection makes no mention of _____.

   (A) Buck's bleeding
   (B) any injury to the man in the red sweater
   (C) Buck's weight

5. The man in the red sweater _____.

   (A) uses both a club and a hatchet as weapons
   (B) seems experienced in dog-breaking
   (C) defeats Buck through luck, rather than skill

6. The selection makes no comparison between Buck and a _____.

   (A) tiger
   (B) devil
   (C) lion

7. In his struggle with the man in the red sweater, Buck demonstrates that he cannot _____.

   (A) learn anything from experience
   (B) take extreme punishment
   (C) bring his rage under control

8. The man in the red sweater can best be described as _____.

   (A) generous and brutal
   (B) shrewd and compassionate
   (C) calm and inhumane

LEARNING NEW WORDS

Line	Word	Meaning	Typical Use
40	**endure** (v.) in-'dyu̇ər	1. bear patiently; suffer	After a while, we asked the children to play outside because we could not *endure* their noise.

		2. continue in the same state; last	The pyramids have *endured* for thousands of years.
		(*ant.* **perish**)	Without water, the desert explorers would surely have *perished*.
42	**ferocity** *(n.)* fə-'räs-ə-tē	fierceness; savage wildness	When the opponents began to use their teeth and fingernails, the fight reached a peak of *ferocity*.
1	**gingerly** *(adv.)* 'jin-jər-lē	very cautiously; with extreme care; timidly	As we were barefoot, we had to step *gingerly* over the sharp pebbles on the way to the water.
6	**grimly** *(adv.)* 'grim-lē	in a cruel and pitiless manner; sternly; harshly	At the opening gong, the fighters moved to the center of the ring and eyed each other *grimly*.
		(*ant.* **tenderly**)	When children fall, some parents sternly rebuke them for carelessness, but others *tenderly* ask if they are hurt.
11	**perch** *(n.)* 'pərch	high place; vantage point; seat; bar or branch on which a bird rests	From her *perch* on the balcony, she was able to observe what went on in the street below.
48	**shrewd** *(adj.)* 'shrüd	clever; cunning	A *shrewd* shopper saves money by taking advantage of special sales.
19	**sufficient** *(adj.)* sə-'fish-ənt	as much as is needed; enough; adequate	A meal adequate for some adults may not be *sufficient* for a hungry teenager.
		(*ant.* **insufficient**)	The money Jack had saved was *insufficient* for the trip; he needed forty dollars more.
4	**tormentor** *(n.)* tȯr-'ment-ər	one who *torments* (causes extreme pain or vexation); persecutor; torturer	Olga used to start fights with her sisters, pull their hair, and even scratch and bite; she was their *tormentor*.
50	**utterly** *(adv.)* 'ət-ər-lē	totally; absolutely; to an extreme degree	The cold and the rain made our hiking trip *utterly* miserable.
49	**withhold** *(v.)* with-'hōld	hold back; refuse to give; retain	The customer may *withhold* the final payment for the repairs until they are satisfactorily completed.
		(*ant.* **grant**)	One hundred and ninety-one diplomas were *granted,* and two were withheld.

Exercise 10.2: Sentence Completion

Which of the two choices correctly completes the sentence? Write the *letter* of your answer in the space provided.

1. You must be utterly exhausted, since you seem to have _____ of energy left.

   A. plenty   B. not a bit

2. The workers came in to warm themselves before the fire; they could not endure the _____.

   A. heat   B. cold

3. My favorite perch was _____.

   A. spaghetti and meatballs   B. the limb of an old apple tree

4. If you withhold these details, _____ will know about them.

   A. everyone   B. no one

5. People without sufficient funds are often compelled to become _____.

   A. lenders   B. borrowers

6. Who would have expected such ferocity from so _____ a youngster as Sandy?

   A. gentle   B. wild

7. Francine _____ that we are planning a surprise for her; she is very shrewd.

   A. must suspect   B. does not know

8. The movers were _____; they lifted the costly furniture gingerly.

   A. careless   B. careful

9. One student, in particular, was my tormentor; he would always _____.

   A. call me names   B. help me with my homework

10. This story grimly reminds us that _____.

   A. good times are coming   B. war is horrible

Exercise 10.3: Definitions

Each expression below defines a word taught on pages 123–124. Enter that word in the space provided.

_____ **1.** as much as is needed

_____ **2.** in a cruel and pitiless manner

_____ **3.** hold back

_____ **4.** one who causes extreme pain

_____ **5.** with extreme care

_____ **6.** high place

_____ **7.** savage wildness

_____ **8.** bear patiently

_____ **9.** marked by cleverness

_____ **10.** to an extreme degree

Exercise 10.4: Synonyms and Antonyms

A. Replace each italicized word with a SYNONYM from the vocabulary list below.

_____ **1.** Fearful of cutting himself, Joel handled his father's razor *timidly*.

_____ **2.** The bulb did not fit my flashlight; it was *totally* useless to me.

_____ **3.** Washington's crossing of the Delaware was a very *clever* move.

_____ **4.** Some of the captives looked upon their guard as a *persecutor*.

_____ **5.** After a while I gave up my *seat* on the stone fence because it was uncomfortable.

B. Replace each italicized word with an ANTONYM from the vocabulary list.

_____ **6.** Many of the new saplings will *perish*.

_____ **7.** Which animals are known for their *tameness?*

_____ **8.** Before pronouncing the verdict, the judge looked *tenderly* at the young prisoner.

_____ **9.** Did your parents *grant* permission for you to go on the ski trip?

_____ **10.** We have *adequate* funds.

Vocabulary List

grimly	endure	ferocity	insufficient	gingerly
utterly	perch	shrewd	tormentor	withhold

Each word in bold type is a *root.* The words below it are its *derivatives.*

endure *(v.)*   I could no longer *endure* her complaints.

endurable *(adj.)*   Her complaints were no longer *endurable.*

endurance *(n.)*   Her complaints were beyond my *endurance.*

ferocious *(adj.)*   The wind was *ferocious.*

ferociously *(adv.)*   It whipped *ferociously* through the trees.

ferocity *(n.)*   I had never seen a wind of such *ferocity.*

grim *(adj.)*   At the goal line we met a *grim* foe.

grimly *(adv.)*   Our opponents were *grimly* determined not to give up an inch of ground.

shrewd *(adj.)*   You were *shrewd.*

shrewdly *(adv.)*   You *shrewdly* avoided the trap.

shrewdness *(n.)*   We admired your *shrewdness.*

sufficient *(adj.)*   Do we have *sufficient* equipment?

sufficiently *(adv.)*   Are we *sufficiently* equipped?

torment *(n.)*   What is the cause of your *torment?*

torment *(v.)*   Is worry about the future *tormenting* you?

tormentor *(n.)*   Is uncertainty your *tormentor?*

utter *(adj.)*   I must have seemed like an *utter* fool.

utterly *(adv.)*   I must have looked *utterly* stupid.

Exercise 10.5: Roots and Derivatives

Fill each blank below with the root or derivative just listed that best completes the sentence.

1. The potatoes were too hard; they had not been _____ boiled.

2. Don't you realize that you are causing your brother extreme pain? Why do you _____ him?

3. The husky watchdogs barked so _____ they seemed like savage beasts.

4. Patricia's _____ surprised me. I did not think she could be so clever.

5. The toothache was _____ at first but, when I began to chew, it became unbearable.

6. The commander looked very _____ as he gave his stern commands.

7. Do you think you would have had the _____ to suffer the hardships that faced the early settlers?

8. Tigers are even more _____ and bloodthirsty than lions.

9. The scene along the path of that tornado was one of _____ destruction. Every building was totally wrecked.

10. Before coming to America, the Puritans suffered _____ and persecution for their religious beliefs.

IMPROVING YOUR SPELLING: FORMING PLURALS

1. For most nouns:

   Add *s* to form the plural.

ear—ears	book—books
eye—eyes	desk—desks

2. For nouns ending in *s, sh, ch,* or *x:*

   Add *es.*

class—classes	bench—benches
dish—dishes	box—boxes

3. For nouns ending in *y* preceded by a *vowel:*

   Add *s.*

day—days	monkey—monkeys
journey—journeys	toy—toys

4. For nouns ending in *y* preceded by a *consonant:*

   Change the *y* to *i* and add *es.*

story—stories	family—families
spy—spies	lady—ladies

5. For a few nouns, neither *s* nor *es* is added, but there is some other change, or changes, in the spelling:

foot—feet	ox—oxen
tooth—teeth	child—children
louse—lice	man—men
mouse—mice	woman—women
goose—geese	

Exercise 10.6: Changing Singular to Plural

The first singular noun has been changed as a sample.

1. city   **cities** _____
2. tree _____
3. driveway _____
4. church _____
5. man _____
6. lamp _____ /
7. candy _____
8. ox _____
9. turkey _____
10. fish _____

11. alley _____
12. toe _____
13. tooth _____
14. fox _____
15. landlady _____
16. gas _____
17. woman _____
18. apple _____
19. play _____
20. pony _____

Exercise 10.7: Changing Plural to Singular

1. lunches   **lunch** _____
2. babies _____
3. lice _____
4. wishes _____
5. children _____

6. highways _____
7. geese _____
8. bodies _____
9. kisses _____
10. keys _____

USING ADVERBS

1. Use an adverb to modify an adjective.

Jack London says that Buck was "*furiously* anxious" to get out of the crate. The adverb *furiously* modifies the adjective *anxious.*

QUESTION: We were (real *or* really) sorry to see you go.

ANSWER: We were *really* sorry to see you go.

EXPLANATION: The adverb *really* is needed to modify the adjective *sorry.* (Note that *real*, in formal English, is an adjective and therefore cannot modify *sorry.* An adjective cannot modify an adjective.)

FURTHER EXAMPLES: She has a *terribly* bad cold. (not *terrible*)
We saw a *remarkably* good movie. (not *remarkable*)

2. Use an adverb to modify a verb.

QUESTION: Your compositions should be written (neat *or* neatly).

ANSWER: Your composition should be written *neatly.*

EXPLANATION: The adverb *neatly* is needed to modify the verb *should be written.* (Note that *neat* is an adjective; an adjective cannot modify a verb.)

FURTHER EXAMPLES: You draw *beautifully.* (not *beautiful*)
Shut the door *quietly.* (not *quiet*)

3. Use an adverb to modify another adverb.

QUESTION: She returned (surprising *or* surprisingly) quickly.

ANSWER: She returned *surprisingly* quickly.

EXPLANATION: The adverb *surprisingly* is needed to modify the adverb *quickly.* (Note that *surprising* is an adjective; an adjective cannot modify an adverb.)

FURTHER EXAMPLES: The baby screams *frightfully* loudly. (not *frightful*)
You finished *unusually* early. (not *unusual*)

4. Remember to use an adjective after certain verbs when they have about the same meaning as *is, are,* etc.

QUESTION: The food tastes (delicious *or* deliciously).

ANSWER: The food tastes *delicious.*

EXPLANATION: The verb *tastes* in this sentence has the meaning of *is,* so we may read the sentence as "The food *is* delicious." Therefore we need the adjective *delicious* to modify the noun *food.*

FURTHER EXAMPLES: The roses smell *sweet.* (not *sweetly*)
This sounds *strange.* (not *strangely*)
The soldier looked *angry.* (not *angrily*)

Exercise 10.8: Using Adjectives and Adverbs
Complete the sentence.

1. We saw an _____ large turtle. *(unbelievable, unbelievably)*

2. This work should be done more _____. *(careful, carefully)*

3. It was a _____ fine birthday party. *(real, really)*

4. Jim _____ knows the answer. *(sure, surely)*

5. The milk tastes _____. *(sour, sourly)*

6. The wind blew _____ fiercely. *(terrible, terribly)*

7. Don't turn the handle so _____. *(rapid, rapidly)*

8. It was _____ dark down there. *(awful, awfully)*

9. The air smelled _____. *(foul, foully)*

10. The elevator rides _____ smoothly. *(remarkable, remarkably)*

Question: Why does Jack London choose red as the color of the sweater of Buck's tormentor (page 121, line 2)?

Answer: Red is the color that best fits in with the savage and brutal nature of that person.

Note that London makes seven references to redness: "red sweater" (lines 2 and 16); "red-eyed devil" (lines 18 and 21); "blood-shot eyes" (line 23); "blood" (line 37); and "bloody" (line 39).

Important. A particular color is not necessarily tied to one impression. Red, for example, is associated with savagery in London's passage, but on other occasions it may be a symbol of love, warmth, welcome, friendliness, danger, etc.

Exercise 10.9: Understanding the Use of Color

Reread the first ten lines of the passage from *The Most Dangerous Game* on page 68. Then answer these questions:

(1) What color predominates in those ten lines?

ANSWER: _____

(2) Why does Richard Connell use that color?

ANSWER: _____

_____

(3) How many references to that color does Connell make in those ten lines?

ANSWER: _____

Exercise 10.10: Describing a Scene

In about three or four sentences, describe a scene, using at least three references to a particular color.

Hints for Topics: a snowfall, a blackout, fog, a room, a house, a building, a wedding, a sunrise, a sunset, a cloudy day, Halloween, St. Valentine's Day, St. Patrick's Day

Sample: A Snowfall

> **When I awoke and looked out the window, huge flakes were swiftly falling, covering the streets, the trees, and the rooftops with thick blankets of white. Surprisingly, the forecast had said nothing about snow.**

(Note the color references: flakes, white, snow)

Sample: A Cloudy Day

> It was a gloomy day. The gray clouds that arrived in the morning refused to go away. The whole world looked pale.

(Color references: gloomy, gray, clouds, pale)

Below, write your description.

_____

_____

_____

_____

_____

_____

_____

_____

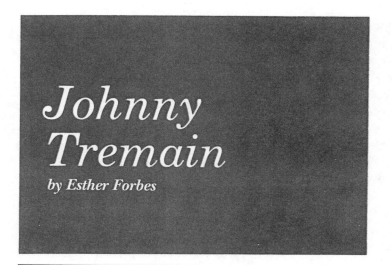

Johnny Tremain

by Esther Forbes

In JOHNNY TREMAIN, *a novel about the American Revolution, Johnny is a young apprentice learning the trade of silversmith from his master, old Mr. Lapham. The following selection shows us what happens to some people when they get old. It also makes us better acquainted with a famous American patriot, John Hancock.*

Johnny slipped into the shop so quietly that Mr. Hancock did not even look up. It was he who owned this great wharf, the warehouses, many of the fine ships tied up along it. He owned sail lofts and shops, and also dwelling houses standing at the head of the
5 wharf. He owned the Lapham house. He was the richest man in New England. Such a wealthy patron might lift the Laphams from poverty to affluence.

Mr. Hancock was comfortably seated in the one armchair which was kept in the shop for patrons. (When I'm master, thought
10 Johnny, there are going to be two armchairs—and I'll sit in one.)

Unobtrusively Johnny got his notebook and pencil. Dove and Dusty were paralyzed into complete inaction. "Do something," Johnny muttered to them, determined his master's shop should look busy. Dusty could not take his eyes off the green velvet coat,
15 sprigged white waistcoat, silver buttons and buckles on the great man, but he picked up a soldering iron and nervously dropped it.

". . . and to be done next Monday—a week from today," Mr. Hancock was saying. "I want it as a birthday present to my venerable Aunt Lydia Hancock. This is the creamer of the set. Only
20 this morning a clumsy maid melted the sugar basin. I want you to make me a new one. I want it about so high . . . so broad . . ."

Johnny glanced at the delicate, lace-ruffled, gesturing hands, guessed the inches, and wrote it down.

Mr. Lapham was looking down at his own gnarled fingers. He nodded and said nothing. He did not even glance at the cream pitcher as Mr. Hancock set it down on a workbench. Johnny's hard, delicate hands, so curiously strong and mature for his age, reached quickly to touch the beautiful thing. It was almost as much by touch as by sight he judged fine silver. It was indeed old-fashioned, more elaborate than the present mode. The garlands on it were rounded out in repoussé work. Mr. Lapham would have to do the repousséing. Johnny hadn't been taught that. He looked at the handle. A sugar basin would have to have two such handles and they would be larger than the one on the creamer. He'd shape it in wax, make a mold. He had cast hundreds of small things since he had gone to work for Mr. Lapham, but nothing so intricate and beautiful as the woman with folded wings whose body formed the handle. He thought he had never seen anything quite so enchanting as this pitcher. It must have been the work of one of the great smiths of forty or fifty years ago. Although he had not intended to address Mr. Hancock, he had said, before he thought, "John Coney, sir?"

Mr. Hancock turned to him. He had a handsome face, a little worn, as though either his health was bad or he did not sleep well.

"Look at the mark, boy."

Johnny turned it over, expecting to see the familiar rabbit of the great Mr. Coney. Instead, there was a pellet, and "L," and a pellet.

"Your master made that creamer—forty years ago. He made the entire set."

"*You* made it!" He had never guessed there had been a time when Mr. Lapham could do such beautiful work.

Line 24. *gnarled:* deformed

Line 31. *repoussé work:* patterns made by hammering

Line 47. *pellet:* little ball

UNDERSTANDING THE SELECTION

Exercise 11.1: Close Reading

In the blank space, write the *letter* of the choice that best completes the statement or answers the question.

1. Mr. Hancock orders a _____ as a present for his aunt.

   (A) creamer
   (B) sugar basin
   (C) teapot

2. The passage suggests that Mr. Lapham _____.

    (A) runs a busy shop
    (B) owns the house he lives in
    (C) is not doing well in business

3. As the result of Mr. Hancock's visit, Johnny's respect for _____ increases greatly.

    (A) Mr. Lapham
    (B) Mr. Hancock
    (C) John Coney

4. When Mr. Hancock describes what he wants to be done, _____.

    (A) Johnny is sure he can do it without help
    (B) Mr. Lapham is eager to take the order
    (C) Johnny decides he can do the work with his master's help

5. The passage suggests that _____.

    (A) Mr. Hancock has no worries at all
    (B) Johnny is the real boss of the shop
    (C) Mr. Lapham is still doing outstanding work

6. The cream pitcher that Mr. Hancock brings in _____.

    (A) has been damaged by a clumsy maid
    (B) has two handles
    (C) is made of silver

7. Which of the following statements is NOT true? _____

    (A) Mr. Hancock owns the ships docked at his wharf.
    (B) Johnny is not in the shop when Mr. Hancock arrives.
    (C) The events of the passage occur on a Monday.

8. The passage describes the _____ of Mr. Hancock, Mr. Lapham, and Johnny.

    (A) speech
    (B) hands
    (C) dress

LEARNING NEW WORDS

Line	Word	Meaning	Typical Use
7	**affluence** (n.) ′af-ˌlü-əns	wealth; riches; abundance of property	The employee came into sudden *affluence* when he won five million dollars in the state lottery.

		(ant. **poverty**)	In the usual success story, the main character rises from *poverty* to riches.
13	**determined** *(adj.)* di-'tər-mənd	resolved; firmly decided; firm	Ms. Walker has turned down every offer to buy her house; she is *determined* not to sell.
30	**elaborate** *(adj.)* i-'lab-ə-rət	having many details; carried out with great care; complicated; detailed	Henry always orders a dish of vanilla ice cream, but I prefer something more *elaborate*, like a chocolate fudge sundae deluxe.
12	**inaction** *(n.)* in-'ak-shən	lack of action or activity; idleness	The mayor promised to have the playground improved but has not done anything about it. We are disappointed at his *inaction*.
41	**intend** *(v.)* in-'tend	have in mind as a purpose or aim; mean; plan	The batter whom I hit with a pitched ball knows that I did not *intend* to do so.
27	**mature** *(adj.)* mə-'tyu̇ər	grown-up; fully developed; adult	For the position of manager, employers will probably not hire a teenager; they usually look for someone more *mature*.
		(ant. **immature, childish**)	For a long time, eighteen-year-olds were unable to vote in national elections because they were considered *immature*.
30	**mode** *(n.)* 'mōd	prevailing style; fashion	Very long skirts were the *mode* in the 1890's.
6	**patron** *(n.)* 'pā-trən	regular customer; client; one who gives support to a person, institution, or cause	We always shop at the Village Grocers. We are among their best *patrons*.
11	**unobtrusively** *(adv.)* ‚ən-əb-'trü-siv-lē	without thrusting oneself forward; inconspicuously; unnoticeably	Carl entered so *unobtrusively* that for a while I was unaware he was present.
		(ant. **obtrusively, noticeably**)	It was impossible not to notice the medals and ribbons *obtrusively* displayed on the monarch's uniform.

| 18–19 | **venerable** *(adj.)* | deserving respect because of age, character, or accomplishments | A special celebration is being planned for the eighty-fifth birthday of our *venerable* grandfather. |
| | 'ven-ər-əbəl | | |

APPLYING WHAT YOU HAVE LEARNED

Exercise 11.2: Sentence Completion

Which of the two choices correctly completes the sentence? Write the *letter* of your answer in the space provided.

1. Since the boys were determined to wait, I had _____ getting them to leave.

   A. little trouble   B. a hard time

2. They are patrons of the Ideal Bake Shop; they _____.

   A. buy there regularly   B. bake the rolls

3. These venerable trees are at least _____ years old.

   A. seven   B. seventy

4. You can see the latest spring modes in _____.

   A. a walk through the woods   B. department-store windows

5. People of affluence _____ low-cost housing.

   A. are not in need of   B. urgently require

6. If you look mature, you may be _____ admission to the movies at the children's rate.

   A. denied   B. granted

7. The dress fits Jane, but she dislikes the complicated flower pattern. She would like something _____ elaborate.

   A. more   B. less

8. Your inaction made us think that you must be _____.

   A. busy   B. lazy

9. Since you ask what I intended, let me tell you what I _____

   A. heard   B. planned

10. Marilyn left unobtrusively; we _____ that she was gone.

    A. didn't even realize   B. noticed at once

Reading Selection 11: Johnny Tremain   *137*

Exercise 11.3: Definitions

Each expression below defines a word taught on pages 135–137. Enter that word in the space provided.

_____ 1. regular customer

_____ 2. deserving respect because of age

_____ 3. abundance of property

_____ 4. prevailing style

_____ 5. having many details

_____ 6. without thrusting oneself forward

_____ 7. fully developed

_____ 8. have in mind as a purpose

_____ 9. firmly decided

_____ 10. lack of activity

Exercise 11.4: Synonyms and Antonyms

Fill the blanks in column A with the required synonyms or antonyms, selecting them from column B.

	Column A	Column B
_____	1. synonym for *detailed*	venerable
_____	2. antonym for *noticeably*	patron
_____	3. synonym for *old*	mode
_____	4. synonym for *resolved*	unobtrusively
_____	5. antonym for *poverty*	mature
_____	6. synonym for *fashion*	elaborate
_____	7. antonym for *childish*	intend
_____	8. synonym for *customer*	affluence
_____	9. synonym for *mean*	inaction
_____	10. antonym for *activity*	determined

Each word in bold type is a *root*. The words below it are its *derivatives*.

affluent *(adj.)*   Many *affluent* persons are present.

affluently *(adv.)*   They are *affluently* dressed.

affluence *(n.)*   They are persons of *affluence*.

determine *(v.)*   Once we *determine* on a plan, we do not change our minds.

determined *(adj.)*   Let us be *determined*.

determinedly *(adv.)*   Let us pursue our goal *determinedly*.

determination *(n.)*   Let us move ahead with *determination*.

elaborate *(v.)*   If you want more details, I will be glad to *elaborate*.

elaborate *(adj.)*   I will give you *elaborate* information.

elaborately *(adv.)*   You will be *elaborately* informed.

inactive *(adj.)*   In the winter, the committee was *inactive*.

inaction *(n.)*   Nothing was done; it was a period of *inaction*.

inactivity *(n.)*   It was a time of *inactivity*.

intend *(v.)*   You know what I *intend* to do.

intention *(n.)*   You know my *intention*.

mature *(adj.)*   Why don't you act grown-up? Be *mature!*

mature *(v.)*   When are you going to *mature?*

maturely *(adv.)*   Why don't you behave more *maturely?*

maturity *(n.)*   Why don't you show some *maturity?*

patron *(n.)*   My brother and I are *patrons* of Joe's Pizza Parlor.

patronize *(v.)*   We *patronize* Joe's Pizza Parlor.

unobtrusive *(adj.)*   I tried to keep in the background; I was *unobtrusive*.

unobtrusively *(adv.)*   I remained *unobtrusively* on the sidelines.

venerate *(v.)*   In some societies, people *venerate* the elderly.

venerable *(adj.)*   They regard the aged as *venerable*.

veneration *(n.)*   They treat the elderly with *veneration*.

Exercise 11.5: Roots and Derivatives

Fill each blank below with the root or derivative just listed that best completes the sentence.

1. Frank is _____; he does not thrust himself forward to gain attention.

2. The Wildcats have not played for the past three weeks. Why have they been _____?

3. My uncle owns a good deal of property and is quite _____.

4. We want a detailed description of what happened; please _____.

5. Fred thought I meant to make fun of him, but that was not my _____.

6. Some people treat their elderly relatives with _____, while others show them no special respect.

7. If you continue to act childishly, people will think that you lack _____.

8. Under proper conditions, a maple sapling will _____ into a beautiful shade tree.

9. Alice is firmly resolved to stay in the dancing contest. I admire her courage and _____.

10. We used to shop at the Ace Supermarket, but now we _____ McGraw and Sons.

Exercise 11.6: Similar or Related Words

Add a word similar in meaning to the other words or expressions. (*Hint:* See page 139.) The first word has been added as a sample.

1. in a grown-up way; in an adult fashion __**mature**_____

2. resolve; make up one's mind firmly _____

3. wealthily; in a rich manner _____

4. do business with; be a regular customer of _____

5. full development; adulthood _____

6. in a complicated way; with many details _____

7. not pushing; not inclined to thrust oneself forward _____

8. regard with deep respect; admire _____

9. firmly; in a resolved manner _____

10. work out in detail; give additional details _____

IMPROVING YOUR SPELLING: ADDING *-ER* AND *-EST* TO ADJECTIVES

1. The suffix *-er* added to an adjective means **"more"**:

   rich + er = richer (more rich)

   Mr. Hancock was *richer* than Mr. Lapham.

2. The suffix *-est* added to an adjective means **"most"**:

   rich + est = richest (most rich)

   Mr. Hancock was the *richest* man in Boston.

3. When adding *-er* and *-est* to adjectives, remember to apply three spelling rules that we have already studied:

   (a) If the adjective ends in silent *e,* drop the *e* before adding *-er* or *-est.*

   large + er = larger
   fierce + est = fiercest

   (b) If the adjective ends in *-y* preceded by a consonant, change *y* to *i* before adding *-er* or *-est.*

   happy + er = happier
   easy + est = easiest

   (c) If the adjective consists of *one syllable* ending in *one consonant* preceded by *one vowel,* double the final consonant before adding *-er* or *-est.*

   fat + er = fatter
   thin + est = thinnest

   Altogether, an adjective has three forms: (1) the simple form *(rich);* (2) the *-er* form *(richer);* and (3) the *-est* form *(richest).*

Exercise 11.7: The Three Forms of an Adjective

On each line below, only one form appears. Fill in the two missing forms as in the first line below.

Simple Form	-ER Form	-EST Form
1. **old**	older	**oldest**
2. ugly		
3.		closest
4.	prettier	
5. blue		

6. _____	_____	gloomiest
7. _____	simpler	_____
8. hot	_____	_____
9. _____	_____	earliest
10. _____	bigger	_____
11. clumsy	_____	_____
12. _____	_____	warmest
13. _____	lonelier	_____
14. slim	_____	_____
15. _____	_____	tiniest
16. _____	cleverer	_____
17. gray	_____	_____
18. _____	_____	humblest
19. _____	greener	_____
20. gentle	_____	_____

USING THE POSSESSIVE OF NOUNS

The *possessive* is the form of a noun that indicates ownership or possession.

The italicized nouns in the phrases below are *possessives:*

    (1) *Johnny's* hands (the hands of Johnny)
    (2) *students'* money (money owned by the students)
    (3) *women's* rights (rights possessed by women)
    (4) the *girls'* names (the names of the girls)

Notice that by using possessives we are able to express ourselves in fewer words. For example, the five-word phrase "money owned by the students" can be reduced to two words: "students' money."

Why do some possessives end in 'S *(Johnny's, women's)* while others end in S' *(students', girls')?* For the answer to this important question, study the following:

1. **If the possessor is a singular noun, add 's.**

    "the hands of **Johnny**" becomes "**Johnny's** hands"
    "the hat owned by the **lady**" becomes "the **lady's** hat"
    "the nest of the **bird**" becomes "the **bird's** nest"
    "books belonging to **Charles**" becomes "**Charles's** books"

2. **If the possessor is a plural noun that ends in s, add only an apostrophe.**

"the hats owned by the **ladies**" becomes "the **ladies'** hats"
"the nest of the **birds**" becomes "the **birds'** nest"

3. **If the possessor is a plural noun that does not end in s, add 's.**

"rights possessed by **women**" becomes "**women's** rights"
"the earnings of **salesmen**" becomes "**salesmen's** earnings"

Exercise 11.8: Conciseness

Reduce each of the following phrases to fewer words by using a possessive.

1. bicycle owned by the girl _____
2. uniforms of the policemen _____
3. toys belonging to the children _____
4. wishes of my parents _____
5. mother of the baby _____
6. duties of secretaries _____
7. jackets for men _____
8. mouth of the horse _____
9. problems facing the city _____
10. the letter James wrote _____

Exercise 11.9: Using Possessives

In the blank space, write the correct form of the noun in parentheses.

1. My _____ name is Jennifer. *(sister)*
2. A _____ job is not an easy one. *(firefighter)*
3. In the early fall, department stores usually have a good selection of girls' and _____ coats. *(women)*
4. Did you notice the sad expression on the _____ face? *(monkey)*
5. The game will be played in the _____ gymnasium. *(boys)*
6. Why are _____ shoes often more expensive than men's? *(ladies)*
7. I remembered the title but forgot the _____ name. *(author)*
8. _____ house is on the next corner. *(Andy)*
9. Dad asked the usher for the way to the _____ rest room. *(gentlemen)*
10. In their campaign speeches, both candidates promised not to waste the _____ money. *(taxpayers)*

The *topic sentence* of a paragraph is the one that expresses the central thought of that paragraph.

Question: What is the topic sentence of the opening paragraph on page 133?

Answer: **He (Mr. Hancock) was the richest man in New England.**

Note that this is the fifth sentence in the paragraph. The topic sentence does not always have to be the first sentence of the paragraph.

Question: How does Esther Forbes support the above topic sentence?

Answer: In sentences 2, 3, and 4, she gives **reasons**—she tells **why** Mr. Hancock was the richest man in New England. He owned the great wharf, the warehouses, and many fine ships (sentence 2); sail lofts, shops, and dwelling houses (sentence 3); and the Lapham house (sentence 4).

Exercise 11.10: Ending a Paragraph With the Topic Sentence

Write a paragraph in which the topic sentence is the last sentence. Support that paragraph, as Esther Forbes did, with reasons.

Here are some hints for topic sentences:

1. _____ is the best—or worst—season of the year.

2. _____ is my favorite leisure—or sports—activity.

3. _____ is not a good—or bad—time to shop.

4. _____ is the most prosperous city in the state—or country.

Model Paragraph

> There are probably more shoppers on a Saturday afternoon than at any other time of the week. It is a time when parking lots are crowded, stores are congested, and the waiting on checkout lines is intolerably long. Worst of all, the selection is likely to be poor, and you may not find what you came for. Saturday afternoon is not a good time to shop.

Below, write your paragraph.

_____

_____

_____

_____

_____

_____

_____

_____

_____

_____

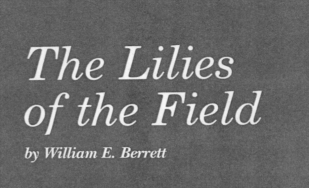

The Lilies of the Field

by William E. Berrett

Homer Smith, a powerful young black Army veteran, becomes involved in helping some nuns build a church. The nuns have no money to pay for materials or labor—only faith that somehow the church will be built.

A Livingston Construction Company truck delivered a thousand bricks on Monday morning. There was no message, no explanation offered. There did not have to be.

"Old man lost a bet with himself," Homer said. "He bet I
5 wouldn't ever do this work. He bet I would be long gone by now."

The new bricks were far superior to any that Homer had laid; regular brickyard adobe, uniform in size and quality. It did not seem right to lay them on the upper levels with the inferior bricks below. The adobe coating, of course, would hide them but Homer
10 considered tearing out the front of the church and using the new bricks there. He didn't mind the work but he decided against it. The people who had brought him bricks when he needed them had a right to have their bricks in the church where they were put.

He had more bricks now than he had hoped for and he decided
15 to build his church higher. That would change the proportions but it would be more impressive. He had a driving urgency in him, a sense of time that he had not had earlier. Time had not mattered; now it did. He did not try to reason why.

The helpful Spanish brought him logs for his roof beams and
20 they were more of a problem than ever. They were his friends and they were all over the place. Whatever they should be doing to make a living was obviously being neglected, but his blunt query— "Shouldn't you be doing something else somewhere?"—brought only shrugs and grins. They had developed a religious fervor and

25 the finishing of the church had become important to them. They
refused to accept the idea that it was his church.

Line 7. *adobe:* sun-dried clay

UNDERSTANDING THE SELECTION

Exercise 12.1: Close Reading

In the blank space, write the *letter* of the choice that best completes the statement.

1. The one thousand bricks were delivered __B__.

   (A) for a reason that was difficult to understand
   (B) because Homer had shown he was not a quitter
   (C) because they had been ordered and paid for

2. The materials for building the church were contributed by __A~B__

   (A) several people
   (B) the Spanish people
   (C) the owner of a construction company

3. Homer did not want to tear down and rebuild the front of the church because __a__.

   (A) it would hurt the feelings of some people
   (B) there would be no advantage in it
   (C) it would be too much work

4. The passage suggests that Homer __a__.

   (A) was in no hurry to finish the church
   (B) needed help with the bricklaying
   (C) felt the Spanish had undergone a change

5. The Spanish wanted to help finish the church because __a__.

   (A) of their friendship for Homer
   (B) they had become very religious
   (C) they had contributed the logs and most of the bricks

6. The passage shows that Homer had been confronted with __B__.

   (A) a labor shortage
   (B) no shortage of any kind
   (C) a materials shortage

7. The delivery of the new bricks altered Homer's plans for the __B__ of the church.

   (A) width
   (B) front
   (C) height

8. The finishing of the church had become important to ___B___ .

    (A) the construction company owner, Homer, and the Spanish
    (B) Homer and the Spanish
    (C) the construction company owner and Homer

LEARNING NEW WORDS

Line	Word	Meaning	Typical Use
22	**blunt** *(adj.)* 'blənt	1. frank; outspoken; plain-spoken and abrupt	When I asked Mitchell if he would lend me his notes, he responded with a *blunt* "No!"
		2. not sharp; dull	The forward edge of the lawn-mower blade is very sharp, but the rear edge is *blunt*.
		(*ant.* **sharp, keen**)	A new razor blade has a *keen* edge.
24	**fervor** *(n.)* 'fər-vər	great warmth of feeling; enthusiasm	When the home team has a bad season, the *fervor* of its supporters cools noticeably.
16	**impressive** *(adj.)* im-'pres-iv	stirring deep feeling; moving; making a marked impression	Alice was very *impressive* as the heroine; the audience was deeply moved.
8	**inferior** *(adj.)* in-'fir-ē-ər	worse; of less value; lower; not so good	Though the melon looked better than the one we had yesterday, it was *inferior* in flavor.
		(*ant.* **superior**)	As far as speed is concerned, the airplane is *superior* to all other modes of travel.
22	**neglect** *(v.)* ni-'glekt	give little attention or care to; disregard	Reggie spends so much time with his motorbike that he is *neglecting* his friends.
		(*ant.* **cherish**)	The fact that I always telephone you, and you never call me back, shows that you do not *cherish* my friendship.
22	**obviously** *(adv.)* 'äb-vē-əs-lē	plainly; evidently; very clearly	The sky darkened and thunder sounded close by; *obviously*, it was going to rain.

7	**quality** (*n.*) 'kwäl-ə-tē	degree of excellence; grade	Foods labeled "Fancy" are supposed to be higher in *quality* than those labeled "Choice."
22	**query** (*n.*) 'kwi(ə)r-ē	question; inquiry to be answered	You have not yet answered my *query*.
		(*ant.* **reply, answer**)	I sent in my question a week ago, but I have not yet received a *reply*.
7	**uniform** (*adj.*) 'yü-nə-ˌfòrm	unchanging; regular; all alike	Are the pearls of *uniform* size, or do they vary?
		(*ant.* **varying**)	The students in our class are alike in age, but they have *varying* interests and abilities.
16	**urgency** (*n.*) 'ər-jən-sē	need for immediate action; stress; pressure	Why are you rushing? We have plenty of time to get there. There is no *urgency*.

APPLYING WHAT YOU HAVE LEARNED

Exercise 12.2: Sentence Completion

Which of the two choices correctly completes the sentence? Write the *letter* of your answer in the space provided.

1. Denise talks about modern music with such fervor that you can see she ____ the subject.

   A. hates   B. enjoys

2. The candidate was so impressive in his first speech that many of us ____.

   A. decided to vote for him   B. thought he was rude

3. Jack had a fine tan when he returned from the weekend; obviously, he had ____.

   A. gotten plenty of sleep   B. been out in the sun

4. The message was of great urgency: ____

   A. "Rush food and medical supplies."   B. "Final examinations have been postponed from May 26 to June 2."

5. Donald's query was ____

   A. "We will never get there on time."   B. "When are we leaving?"

6. The parents have given the child ____ attention; they have not neglected him.

    A. adequate   B. very little

7. The squares on a checkerboard are uniform; they ____ .

    A. vary in size   B. all are the same size

8. You are being blunt if you say to someone who is making up an excuse: ____

    A. "You must be mistaken."   B. "You're a liar."

9. The dungarees I bought last month are inferior; they ____ .

    A. are already worn out   B. look as good as new

10. If your English teacher complains about the quality of your reports, ____ .

    A. you may not have handed in all your reports   B. something may be wrong with the writing, content, or organization of your reports

Exercise 12.3: Conciseness

Which word taught on pages 148–149 can do the work of all the italicized words?

_____   **1.** My cousin's guitar is of a high *degree of excellence.*

_____   **2.** At first, I studied French with *great warmth of feeling.*

_____   **3.** *Very clearly,* I cannot speak if you keep interrupting me.

_____   **4.** George tells the truth, even if it hurts. He is very *plain-spoken and abrupt.*

_____   **5.** The nails in this box are *all alike* in size.

_____   **6.** You should not have alarmed us, since there was no *need for immediate action.*

_____   **7.** Take care that you do not *give little attention to* your health.

_____   **8.** The flavor of this plum is *not so good.*

_____   **9.** If you have any *inquiry to be answered,* raise your hand.

_____   **10.** A barely satisfactory performance, you will admit, is not *deeply stirring.*

Exercise 12.4: Synonyms and Antonyms

A. Replace each italicized word with a SYNONYM from the vocabulary list on the next page.

_____   **1.** I notice that your *enthusiasm* for photography has not cooled.

_____   **2.** The new chairs in the library are of a better *grade.*

_____ 3. Sandra's cousins *evidently* are people of affluence.

_____ 4. Please take care of this at once, as it is a matter of the greatest *stress*.

_____ 5. That was a very *moving* plea.

B. Replace each italicized word with an ANTONYM from the vocabulary list.

_____ 6. A great deal of *superior* merchandise has been placed on sale.

_____ 7. The *reply* was given immediate attention.

_____ 8. If Sue were to get that opportunity, she would probably *cherish* it.

_____ 9. The razor blade was *sharp*.

_____ 10. The salesclerk opened a box of shirts *varying* in size and pattern.

Vocabulary List

inferior	query
blunt	neglect
uniform	quality
obviously	impressive
urgency	fervor

LEARNING SOME ROOTS AND DERIVATIVES

Each word in bold type is a *root*. The words below it are its *derivatives*.

blunt *(adj.)*   I admire you for being *blunt*.

bluntly *(adv.)*   I admire you for speaking *bluntly*.

bluntness *(n.)*   I admire your *bluntness*.

fervent *(adj.)*   The candidate received *fervent* applause.

fervently *(adv.)*   The candidate was *fervently* applauded.

fervor *(n.)*   The candidate was applauded with *fervor*.

impress *(v.)*   Your marks *impress* me.

impressive *(adj.)*   Your school record is *impressive*.

impressively *(adv.)*   You recite *impressively* in class.

impression *(n.)*   All in all, you are making a fine *impression*.

inferior *(adj.)*	What makes you think you are *inferior?*
inferiority *(n.)*	Why are you convinced of your *inferiority?*
neglect *(v.)*	Some drivers *neglect* the maintenance of their cars.
neglect *(n.)*	Their cars show signs of *neglect.*
negligent *(adj.)*	Then there are *negligent* drivers who disregard traffic regulations.
negligently *(adv.)*	They drive *negligently.*
negligence *(n.)*	Their *negligence* causes many accidents.
obvious *(adj.)*	It is *obvious* that you have a cold.
obviously *(adv.)*	*Obviously* you have a cold.
query *(n.)*	What reply would you give to a *query* about your experience?
query *(v.)*	If they *query* you about your experience, what will you say?
uniform *(adj.)*	The students' replies were not *uniform.*
uniformly *(adv.)*	They did not answer *uniformly.*
uniformity *(n.)*	There was no *uniformity* in the students' answers.
urge *(v.)*	I *urge* you to do something.
urgent *(adj.)*	The situation is *urgent.*
urgently *(adv.)*	Your help is *urgently* needed.
urgency *(n.)*	The *urgency* of the situation calls for immediate action.

Exercise 12.5: Roots and Derivatives

Fill each blank below with the root or derivative just listed that best completes the sentence.

1. The situation is _____! We must act at once!

2. It is useless to _____ her, as she refuses to answer any questions.

3. Since you have asked me to be frank, I will speak _____.

4. Don't you agree that variety is more interesting than _____?

5. The first speaker moved us deeply, but the others failed to _____ us.

6. Some of Paula's more _____ admirers continued to applaud her when the rest of the audience had stopped.

7. The flood victims _____ need warm clothing and medical supplies.

8. Sometimes an explanation that may be very clear to some pupils is not _____ to the rest of the class.

9. If you keep saying that my work is worse than anybody else's, you will give me a sense of _____.

10. You must pay strict attention to the safety rules in shop. If you are _____, you may get hurt.

Exercise 12.6: Defining Roots and Derivatives
Enter the word from pages 151–152 that matches each definition below.

1. in an enthusiastic manner   _____

2. failure to exercise required care   _____

3. lack of sharpness   _____

4. in a way that stirs deep feeling   _____

5. in a manner that does not vary   _____

6. press upon one's attention   _____

7. condition of being worse   _____

8. in a carelessly easy way   _____

9. effect produced by stirring deep feeling   _____

10. ask questions   _____

IMPROVING YOUR SPELLING: CAPITALIZING PROPER NOUNS

1. Capitalize **proper nouns** (names of particular persons, places, things, etc.):

> Homer Smith (a particular man)
>
> Salt Lake City (a particular city)
>
> Livingston Construction Company (a particular company)

2. Do not capitalize **common nouns** (nouns that refer to no particular person, place, or thing):

> man   city   company

3. Capitalize the names of the days, months, and holidays. They are proper nouns:

> Monday   February   Independence Day

4. Do not capitalize the names of the seasons. They are considered as common nouns:

> spring   summer   autumn (fall)   winter

5. Capitalize the names of sections of the country. They are proper nouns:

New England   the West   the South   the Northeast

6. Do not capitalize *north, south, east,* and *west* when they indicate direction.

Go two blocks **w**est and one block **n**orth.

Exercise 12.7: Proofreading for Capitalization

Only two of the sentences below are correct. The rest have one or more errors in capitalization. On the line below each sentence, rewrite the misspelled word or words. If the sentence is correct, write "correct."

1. Gerald has relatives in the south.

   _____

2. We go bowling on wednesdays and fridays.

   _____

3. Pat's sister works in a savings bank.

   _____

4. Name a river that flows into the mississippi river.

   _____

5. Do you have an account at the liberty savings bank?

   _____

6. My Parents will return after labor day.

   _____

7. The leaves were beautiful last Autumn.

   _____

8. Is the highway east or west of the canal?

   _____

9. I attended the river road intermediate school.

   _____

10. The Storm is moving North at eighteen miles an hour.

   _____

Learn the difference between these two verbs:

1. To **lie** means to "be in a horizontal position."

Its principal parts are *lie, lay, lain.*

Its present participle is *lying.*

Study these uses of **to lie** and refer to them when in doubt.

PRESENT: The dog *lies* (or *is lying*) on the grass.

FUTURE: The dog *will lie* on the grass.

PAST: The dog *lay* on the grass.

OTHER TENSES:

The dog *has lain* on the grass.

The dog *had lain* on the grass.

The dog *will have lain* on the grass.

2. To **lay** means to "put down."

Its principal parts are *lay, laid, laid.*

Its present participle is *laying.*

Study these uses of **to lay** and refer to them when in doubt.

PRESENT: Homer *lays* (or *is laying*) bricks.

FUTURE: Homer *will lay* bricks.

PAST: Homer *laid* bricks.

OTHER TENSES:

Homer *has laid* bricks.

Homer *had laid* bricks.

Homer *will have laid* bricks.

Exercise 12.8: Using *Lie* or *Lay*?

Complete the sentence.

1. Where should I _____ these packages? *(lie or lay)*
2. For half the night I _____ awake. *(laid or lay)*
3. Where have you _____ my umbrella? *(lain or laid)*
4. The cat was _____ on the rug. *(lying or laying)*

5. It is not so easy to _____ floor tile. *(lie* or *lay)*

6. The treasure still _____ at the bottom of the sea. *(lays* or *lies)*

7. When we came home, you were _____ on the sofa, fast asleep. *(laying* or *lying)*

8. Your notes have _____ on my desk ever since you put them there. *(laid* or *lain)*

9. _____ the new books on the top shelf. *(Lay* or *Lie)*

10. I will _____ down for a nap because I am very tired. *(lay* or *lie)*

IMPROVING YOUR COMPOSITION SKILLS: DISCUSSING A PROBLEM AND ITS SOLUTION

Reread the paragraph in which William E. Barrett discusses a problem that Homer had (page 146, lines 6–13). Note that the paragraph is organized as follows:

THE FIRST THREE SENTENCES explain the problem—the arrival of the new bricks. Homer now had to decide whether or not to rebuild the front of the church with the new bricks.

THE FOURTH SENTENCE explains the decision Homer made—he will not rebuild the front of the church.

THE FIFTH AND LAST SENTENCE tells the reason for that decision—the people who had brought Homer bricks when he needed them had a right to have their bricks in the church where they were put.

Exercise 12.9:   Writing About a Problem

In a paragraph of about five sentences, describe a problem that you—or someone you know—had. Build your paragraph as Barrett did, by discussing the following matters one after the other:

> the problem and its possible solutions
> the solution you chose
> the reason or reasons for your choice

Hints for Topics:

   A problem with someone who takes up too much of your time, or borrows but does not return things

   A problem with people who are noisy—for example, loud talkers in the library; neighbors who play music too loud

   A problem with an animal—a stray dog; a cat that preys on birds, etc.

   A problem with an appliance or gadget—a defective stapler; a camera hard to operate, etc.

Sample Paragraph

Recently, a stray dog wandered into our street and kept barking so fiercely that frightened parents kept their children indoors. Since he would not go away, we had to decide whether or not to feed him. We felt that if we fed him, he might not go back home. Anyhow, on the second day, we put out water and food for him. It was the humane thing to do.

Now write your paragraph.

_____

_____

_____

_____

_____

_____

_____

_____

_____

_____

_____

Review of Unit III

Review III.1: Vocabulary and Spelling

Fill in the missing letters of the *Word*. (Each space stands for one missing letter.)
Then write the *Complete Word* in the blank space.

	Definition	Word	Complete Word
1.	with extreme care	GIN __ __ RLY	_____
2.	false show	PRE __ __ NSE	_____
3.	give little care to	__ __ __ LECT	_____
4.	hold back	WITH __ __ __ D	_____
5.	unusually	__ __ __ EPTIONALLY	_____
6.	stir deep feeling	__ __ PRESS	_____
7.	half of a school year	SE __ __ STER	_____
8.	lack of activity	__ __ ACTION	_____
9.	enthusiasm	FERV __ __	_____
10.	offender	CULP __ __ T	_____
11.	have in mind as a purpose	__ __ TEND	_____
12.	vantage point	PER __ __	_____
13.	requiring immediate attention	__ __ GENT	_____
14.	confused situation	__ __ __ PLICATION	_____
15.	having many details	__ __ __ BORATE	_____
16.	cause extreme pain	T __ __ MENT	_____
17.	degree of excellence	__ __ ALITY	_____
18.	not enough	IN __ __ __ FICIENT	_____
19.	regard with deep respect	V __ __ ERATE	_____
20.	prevailing style	__ OD __	_____

Review III.2: Synonyms

To each line, add a word that has the *same meaning* as the first two words on the line. Choose your words from the vocabulary list.

Vocabulary List

1. totally; absolutely _____   patron

2. firm; determined _____   obvious

3. force; energy _____   outrage

4. outspokenly; frankly _____   shrewd

5. offense; insult _____   core

6. plain; evident _____   resolved

7. center; heart _____   utterly

8. clever; cunning _____   grim

9. customer; client _____   vigor

10. harsh; stern _____   bluntly

Review III.3: Antonyms

For each italicized word in column A, write the best *antonym* from column B.

Column A   *Column B*

_____ 1. *mature* behavior   bland

_____ 2. brief *reply*   childish

_____ 3. *ferocious* animal   poverty

_____ 4. of *varying* quality   query

_____ 5. will not *perish*   tame

_____ 6. greatest *affluence*   noticeable

_____ 7. *superior* material   crude

_____ 8. an *irritating* diet   uniform

_____ 9. made himself *unobtrusive*   inferior

_____ 10. *elegant* manner of speaking   endure

Review III.4: Wordbuilding With Suffixes

Fill each blank with a word formed by adding one of the following suffixes to the word in parentheses:

-ABLE, -IBLE, -ER, -EST, -ITY, -NESS

1. We can rely on Joan; she is _____. *(depend)*
2. The United States is one of the _____ nations in the world. *(wealthy)*
3. My little brother has a great deal of _____ for his age. *(shrewd)*
4. You can record on both sides of the tape; it is _____. *(reverse)*
5. I think that I can become a bit _____ if I avoid fattening foods. *(slim)*
6. Can't you think of a more _____ excuse? *(believe)*
7. Our adviser is a person of experience and _____. *(mature)*
8. The sun was not to be seen. It was one of the _____ mornings of the year. *(gloomy)*
9. You should know that 12/16 is _____ to 3/4. *(reduce)*
10. My low mark on the test gave me a feeling of _____. *(inferior)*

Review III.5: Sentence Completion

Complete each sentence below with the most appropriate word from the following vocabulary list:

Vocabulary List

neglected	vigor	intended
affluence	outrage	inferior
culprit	patron	perch
elaborate	endured	blunt

1. After we had been on line a half-hour, two pupils tried to push in ahead of us, but we wouldn't permit this _____.
2. Why don't you come down from your _____ on the stairs and sit with the rest of us?
3. The new captain has promised to give more attention to matters that were too often _____ in the past.
4. _____ precautions are taken for the safety of visiting heads of state.
5. Are you aware of the risks that the first astronauts _____?
6. It is surprising that _____ goods should often cost as much as first-quality merchandise.
7. After my illness, I was excused from the gym class until I could regain my full _____.

8. I had _____ to pay about ten dollars for a new glove, but I couldn't find a good one at that price.

9. These scissors need to be sharpened; they are very _____.

10. Why do you say I was responsible? I am not the _____.

Review III.6: Roots and Derivatives
On lines B and C, write the required forms of the italicized word on line A.

1. A. Your dog was *ferocious.*

    B. Your dog barked _____.

    C. Your dog barked with _____.

2. A. George's behavior was an *outrage.*

    B. George behaved _____.

    C. George's behavior was _____.

3. A. The apartment was *elegantly* furnished.

    B. The apartment was furnished with _____.

    C. The apartment had _____ furnishings.

4. A. My young brother is an *active* child.

    B. He likes to be _____ involved.

    C. On the other hand, my sister is quite _____.

5. A. I used *blunt* language.

    B. I spoke _____.

    C. I spoke with _____.

6. A. Why do you *torment* us?

    B. Why are you our _____?

    C. Why do you cause us _____?

7. A. The pain was more than I could *endure.*

    B. The pain was beyond my _____.

    C. The pain was not _____.

8. A. Gail is a *fervent* rooter for our team.

    B. Gail _____ roots for our team.

    C. Gail roots for our team with _____.

9. A. Don't *neglect* your teeth.

    B. Don't be _____ about your teeth.

    C. Don't treat your teeth with _____

10. A. How long does it take a sapling to reach *maturity?*

    B. How long does it take a sapling to become _____?

    C. How long does it take a sapling to _____?

11. A. He gave us a *determined* look.

    B. He looked at us _____.

    C. He gave us a look of _____.

12. A. Did my speech make an *impression* on you?

    B. Did my speech _____ you?

    C. Was my speech _____?

13. A. Ralph dealt with the problem *shrewdly.*

    B. Ralph showed _____ in dealing with the problem.

    C. Ralph was _____ in dealing with the problem.

14. A. I don't like to make a *pretense* of knowing the answer.

    B. I don't like to _____.

    C. I don't like to be a _____.

15. A. We are in very *urgent* need of funds.

    B. We need funds very _____.

    C. Our need for funds is of great _____.

16. A. They live in an *affluent* style.

    B. They are people of _____.

    C. They live _____.

17. A. Don't *complicate* matters further.

    B. Don't make matters more _____.

    C. Don't add to the _____.

18. A. He showed *vigor* in defending himself.

    B. He put up a _____ defense.

    C. He defended himself _____.

19. A. We regard heroes with *veneration.*

    B. We _____ heroes.

C. We regard heroes as _____ .

20. A. Their answers were not *uniform.*

    B. They did not answer _____ .

    C. There was no _____ in their answers.

Review III.7: Concise Writing

In the space provided, rewrite the following paragraph to make it more concise. (*Hint:* Reduce each boldfaced expression to a single word.) The first sentence will be rewritten to help you get started.

Something **not to our liking** has occurred—there has been illegal dumping of chemical wastes. This is an **act of violence that shows no regard for other people.** The **individuals who committed this crime** are known. Why are the authorities **refusing to release** their names? Another matter that adds to the public's **extreme annoyance** is the cleanup. The latest word is that it will be delayed because the wastes are dangerous and must be handled **with extreme care.** And who is going to pay for the cleanup? The town's officials seem to be **giving little attention to** this problem. They must think there is no **need for immediate action.**

    Something disagreeable has occurred—there has been illegal dumping of chemical wastes.

_____

_____

_____

_____

_____

_____

_____

_____

_____

_____

_____

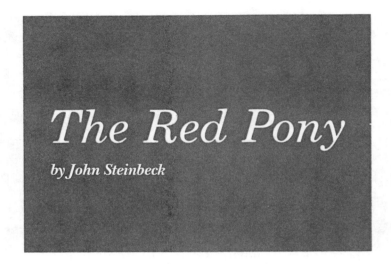

The Red Pony

by John Steinbeck

Have you ever been unfairly punished just because you happened to be around when your parents were having a quarrel?

Jody ran into the kitchen. "We got a letter!" he cried.

His mother looked up from a pan of beans. "Who has?"

"Father has. I saw it in his hand."

Carl strode into the kitchen then, and Jody's mother asked,
5 "Who's the letter from, Carl?"

He frowned quickly. "How did you know there was a letter?"

She nodded her head in the boy's direction. "Big-Britches Jody told me."

Jody was embarrassed.

10 His father looked down at him contemptuously. "He *is* getting to be a Big-Britches," Carl said. "He's minding everybody's business but his own. Got his big nose into everything."

Mrs. Tiflin relented a little. "Well, he hasn't enough to keep him busy. Who's the letter from?"

15 Carl still frowned on Jody. "I'll keep him busy if he isn't careful." He held out a sealed letter. "I guess it's from your father."

Mrs. Tiflin took a hairpin from her head and slit open the flap. Her lips pursed judiciously. Jody saw her eyes snap back and forth
20 over the lines. "He says," she translated, "he says he's going to drive out Saturday to stay for a little while. Why, this is Saturday.

164

The letter must have been delayed." She looked at the postmark. "This was mailed day before yesterday. It should have been here yesterday." She looked up questioningly at her husband, and then

25 her face darkened angrily. "Now what have you got that look on you for? He doesn't come often."

Carl turned his eyes away from her anger. He could be stern with her most of the time, but when occasionally her temper arose, he could not combat it.

30 "What's the matter with you?" she demanded again.

In his explanation there was a tone of apology Jody himself might have used. "It's just that he talks," Carl said lamely. "Just talks."

"Well, what of it? You talk yourself."

35 "Sure I do. But your father only talks about one thing."

"Indians!" Jody broke in excitedly. "Indians and crossing the plains!"

Carl turned fiercely on him. "You get out, Mr. Big-Britches! Go on, now! Get out!"

40 Jody went miserably out the back door and closed the screen with elaborate quietness. Under the kitchen window his shamed, downcast eyes fell upon a curiously shaped stone, a stone of such fascination that he squatted down and picked it up and turned it over in his hands.

45 The voices came clearly to him through the open kitchen window. "Jody's damn well right," he heard his father say. "Just Indians and crossing the plains. I've heard that story about how the horses got driven off about a thousand times. He just goes on and on, and he never changes a word in the things he tells."

Line 10. *contemptuously:* scornfully

UNDERSTANDING THE SELECTION

Exercise 13.1: Close Reading

In the blank space, write the *letter* of the choice that best completes the statement or answers the question.

1. The main reason for Carl's bad temper is that ___a___ .

   (A) Jody is not minding his own business
   (B) he has been scolded by his wife
   (C) Grandfather is coming

2. Mrs. Tiflin believes the main trouble with Jody is that he ___B___ .

   (A) is growing up too fast
   (B) talks too much
   (C) does not have enough to do

3. The selection indicates that, when Grandfather tells his story, Jody finds it ___ . *B*

    (A) too long
    (B) exciting
    (C) boring

4. The following is NOT true of Grandfather's story: ___ *C*

    (A) It always keeps changing.
    (B) It deals with Indians and crossing the plains.
    (C) It has been told many times before.

5. The selection suggests that Jody's ___ . *a*

    (A) father understands him better than does his mother
    (B) parents do not understand him
    (C) mother understands him better than does his father

6. Mrs. Tiflin utters not a word of criticism of ___ . *C*

    (A) Carl
    (B) her father
    (C) Jody

7. What triggers Mrs. Tiflin's temper? *A*

    (A) a remark by Jody
    (B) a look on her husband's face
    (C) the letter

8. The selection reveals that ___ . *A*

    (A) Grandfather is a frequent visitor
    (B) Mrs. Tiflin often loses her temper
    (C) the letter was mailed on Thursday

LEARNING NEW WORDS

Line	Word	Meaning	Typical Use
31	**apology** (n.) ə-'päl-ə-jē	admission of a fault with a plea for pardon; expression of regret for an offense or discourtesy; excuse	I admit I was wrong when I called you a liar. Please accept my *apology*.
29	**combat** (v.) kəm-'bat	struggle against; oppose vigorously; battle (*ant.* **defend**)	We must do all we can to *combat* hunger, disease, and ignorance.

9	**embarrass** *(v.)* im-'bar-əs	make ill at ease; cause to feel self-conscious; fluster	It *embarrassed* me deeply to discover when I came to the cashier that I did not have enough money to pay for my meal.
		(ant. **relieve***)*	I was ill at ease when you thought I had not returned your key, and I was greatly *relieved* by the news that you had found it.
6	**frown** *(v.)* 'fraùn	wrinkle the forehead in anger or annoyance; look with disapproval *(ant.* **smile***)*	I know you didn't like the dessert because you *frowned* when you tasted it.
32	**lamely** *(adv.)* 'lām-lē	1. unsatisfactorily; weakly; in an unconvincing manner	When asked for her homework, Gail *lamely* excused herself by saying she had left it at home.
		2. in a limping manner, as the result of an injury or physical disability; haltingly	For several days after hurting my leg, I walked *lamely,* but I don't limp anymore.
40	**miserably** *(adv.)* 'miz-ə-rə-blē	very unhappily; wretchedly	The winners jumped for joy as the losers crept *miserably* from the field.
28	**occasionally** *(adv.)* ə-'kāzh-ən-əl-ē	sometimes; now and then; once in a while	I used to see my cousins quite often, but now I meet them only *occasionally.*
		(ant. **customarily***)*	*Customarily,* Gregg brings sandwiches from home, but once in a while he buys his lunch at school.
13	**relent** *(v.)* ri-'lent	become less severe; soften; let up	After stating that she would not allow Nick to return to the class, Ms. Krug *relented* and gave him another chance.
18	**slit** *(v.)* 'slit	cut in a straight line; split open by a straight, lengthwise cut	Using a letter opener, the clerk neatly *slit* open the sealed envelopes.
27	**stern** *(adj.)* 'stərn	hard or severe in nature; harsh; strict; unyielding	Once Mr. Burns tells you that you are fired, he will not relent. He is a *stern* employer.

(*ant.* **lenient**)   Parents cannot be *lenient* with children who are reported to have been playing with matches.

Exercise 13.2:   Sentence Completion

Which of the two choices correctly completes the sentence? Write the *letter* of your answer in the space provided.

1. I go to the museum occasionally, about three or four times a _____ .

   A. year   B. week

2. The judge's stern expression shows a determination not to be _____ with the offender.

   A. strict   B. easygoing

3. More funds are needed if we are to combat _____ successfully.

   A. health   B. crime

4. Believing that he had surely _____ , Jonathan gathered his belongings and walked miserably from the examination room.

   A. failed   B. passed

5. To _____ the carton, slit the tape along the dotted lines.

   A. close   B. open

6. After refusing to sell his old bicycle for less than $25, Jeff relented and changed his price to _____ .

   A. $20   B. $30

7. Brenda was embarrassed because she was _____ .

   A. the only one who had not   B. sure that she had not made a
      been given a part in the play   mistake

8. We had expected Phil to make a _____ reply, but he answered lamely.

   A. brief   B. satisfactory

9. We usually are willing to make an apology when we _____ .

   A. want to be forgiven   B. realize that we have done nothing
                                       wrong

10. If your audience frowns, you can see that they are _____ with what you are doing.

    A. pleased   B. annoyed

Exercise 13.3: Definitions

Each expression below defines a word taught on pages 166–168. Enter that word in the space provided.

_____	**1.** once in a while
_____	**2.** in an unconvincing manner
_____	**3.** make ill at ease
_____	**4.** hard and severe in nature
_____	**5.** split open by a lengthwise cut
_____	**6.** expression of regret for an offense
_____	**7.** become less severe
_____	**8.** very unhappily
_____	**9.** struggle against
_____	**10.** look with disapproval

Exercise 13.4: Synonyms and Antonyms

A. Replace each italicized word with a SYNONYM from the vocabulary list below.

_____	**1.** Are they sticking to their demands, or have they *softened*?
_____	**2.** Please listen to my *excuse*.
_____	**3.** Asked why he had missed the last three meetings, Barry replied *unconvincingly*, "I had to go somewhere."
_____	**4.** Some of the pages in the magazine had not been *cut* open.
_____	**5.** We suffered *wretchedly*.

Vocabulary List

lamely	relented
frowned	occasionally
combatted	apology
slit	miserably
embarrassed	stern

B. Replace each italicized word with an ANTONYM from the vocabulary list.

_____ **6.** I was greatly *relieved* by your comment.

_____ **7.** Have any manufacturers in your area ever *defended* pollution?

_____ **8.** Bruce *customarily* forgets his keys.

_____ **9.** Some parents are too *lenient* with their children.

_____ **10.** When I told Marie what you had said, she *smiled*.

LEARNING SOME ROOTS AND DERIVATIVES

Each word in bold type is a *root.* The words below it are its *derivatives.*

apology *(n.)*	I accepted her *apology.*
apologetic *(adj.)*	She was very *apologetic.*
apologetically *(adv.)*	She spoke very *apologetically.*
apologize *(v.)*	She was eager to *apologize.*
combat *(v.)*	The people were not prepared to *combat* an invader.
combat *(n.)*	They had no training in *combat.*
combative *(adj.)*	They were not a *combative* people.
combatant *(n.)*	They had never been *combatants.*
embarrass *(v.)*	Lies can *embarrass* you.
embarrassing *(adj.)*	It is *embarrassing* to be caught in a lie.
embarrassingly *(adv.)*	Truth has a way of *embarrassingly* exposing a liar.
embarrassment *(n.)*	Avoid possible *embarrassment.* Don't tell lies.
frown *(v.)*	If you *frown,* I know you are displeased.
frown *(n.)*	Your *frown* shows you are dissatisfied.
lame *(adj.)*	Our dog has been *lame* since her accident.
lamely *(adv.)*	She has been hopping *lamely* on three legs.
lameness *(n.)*	We hope her *lameness* will gradually disappear.
misery *(n.)*	The fans departed in *misery.*
miserable *(adj.)*	They were *miserable* over our defeat.
miserably *(adv.)*	They *miserably* returned to their homes.

occasion (n.)	Parties are not an everyday *occasion.*
occasional (adj.)	We have an *occasional* party.
occasionally (adv.)	*Occasionally*, we have a party.
slit (v.)	My sister accidentally *slit* the tablecloth.
slit (n.)	My sister accidentally made a *slit* in the tablecloth.
stern (adj.)	Sometimes you have to be *stern.*
sternly (adv.)	Sometimes you must speak *sternly.*
sternness (n.)	Occasionally, *sternness* is necessary.

Exercise 13.5: Roots and Derivatives

Fill each blank with the root or derivative just listed that best completes the sentence.

1. Many were wounded in the fierce _____.

2. I should have been very happy; instead, I was _____.

3. I noticed that your cat limps a little. What is the cause of her _____?

4. I refuse to _____ because I am not sorry for what I have done.

5. Our teacher has said that he cannot be right all of the time, since he may make a(n) _____ mistake.

6. Your _____ shows that you are annoyed with me.

7. Vincent should have asked to be forgiven for his rudeness, but he was not at all _____.

8. Debbie made a(n) _____ in the mask for the mouth, another for the nose, and two more for the eyes.

9. Some students feel ill at ease in making a speech until they learn to overcome their _____.

10. I had always regarded Mr. Green as a lenient teacher until he scolded me very _____.

Exercise 13.6: Defining Roots and Derivatives

Enter the word from pages 170–171 that matches the definition below.

1. wretchedness _____

2. battler; one who struggles _____

3. straight, lengthwise cut _____

4. look of annoyance _____

5. limping _____

6. strictness _____

7. eager to battle or struggle _____

8. making one ill at ease _____

9. regretfully _____

10. a particular time _____

IMPROVING YOUR SPELLING: TROUBLESOME CONSONANTS

Before discussing this topic, let us review: *a, e, i, o,* and *u* are ***vowels;*** all the other letters of the alphabet are ***consonants.***

Some of us have trouble with the consonants in certain words. For example, we may not be sure of the exact number of *r*'s and *s*'s in *embarrass,* or *c*'s and *s*'s in *occasion.*

Words with such troublesome consonants should be grouped in a way that will make learning easier.

Study these three groups.

1. THE 2 + 2 GROUP

Every word in this group has a troublesome *doubled* consonant followed by another troublesome *doubled* consonant:

embarrass   misspell   possess

2. THE 2 + 1 GROUP

Every word in this group has a troublesome *doubled* consonant followed by a troublesome *single* consonant:

occasion   bulletin   apparel

3. THE 1 + 2 GROUP

Every word in this group has a troublesome *single* consonant followed by a troublesome *doubled* consonant:

necessary   recommend   sheriff

Exercise 13.7: Grouping Words With Troublesome Consonants

Put each of the following words into its proper group below:

buffalo	tariff	Tennessee	aggression	accumulate
satellite	tomorrow	Caribbean	vaccinate	committee
parallel	moccasin	access	beginning	assassinate

$\boxed{2 + 2}$

$\boxed{2 + 1}$

$\boxed{1 + 2}$

_____   _____   _____

_____   _____   _____

_____   _____   _____

_____   _____   _____

_____   _____   _____

_____   _____   _____

Exercise 13.8: Proofreading for Spelling

On most of the lines below, one word has been misspelled. Write that word correctly in the space at the right. If there are no errors on the line (there are two correct lines), write *correct*.

1. beggining, accumulation, tariff _____

2. assassination, tommorow, vaccinate _____

3. committee, buffalo, neccessarily _____

4. embarrassing, possesion, parallel _____

5. occasional, unnecessarily, accumulated _____

6. mispelled, bulletin, occasionally _____

7. moccasin, sheriff, reccomendation _____

8. vaccination, sattelite, misspelling _____

9. unnecessary, apparel, Carribean _____

10. Tennessee, access, embarrassment _____

PUNCTUATING DIRECT QUOTATIONS

1. Use quotation marks to set off a *direct* quotation (the exact words of the speaker) from the rest of the sentence:

    Mrs. Tiflin said, "Jody hasn't enough to keep him busy."

2. Use *no* quotation marks if the sentence contains an *indirect* quotation:

    Mrs. Tiflin said that Jody hasn't enough to keep him busy.

3. If the direct quotation is a question, use a question mark *inside* the closing quotation mark:

    "What's the matter with you?" she demanded again.

4. If the direct quotation is an exclamation, use an exclamation point *inside* the closing quotation mark:

    "We got a letter!" Jody cried.

5. Use a comma to separate a direct quotation from the rest of the sentence:

    "It's just that he talks," Carl said lamely.
    Carl said lamely, "It's just that he talks."

Note that *no comma is needed* if the direct quotation is already separated from the rest of the sentence by a question mark or an exclamation point, as in 3 and 4 above.

Exercise 13.9: Proofreading for Punctuation

Rewrite each sentence, supplying all required punctuation. The first one has been done for you as an example.

1. You may borrow my book I told the new pupil

    "You may borrow my book," I told the new pupil.

2. Carl asked How did you know there was a letter

    _____

3. Indians Jody broke in excitedly

    _____

4. Jane's father said that he would take us in his car

    _____

5. Who called while I was out my sister queried

    _____

6. Carl shouted fiercely You get out

_____

7. Suddenly someone behind me screamed Help

_____

8. Have you anything further to say the judge inquired

_____

9. The defendant replied I wish to state that I am innocent

_____

10. Hitch your wagon to a star said Ralph Waldo Emerson

_____

IMPROVING YOUR COMPOSITION SKILLS: USING CONVERSATION

In lines 5–9 on page 164, John Steinbeck writes:

> Jody's mother asked, "Who's the letter from, Carl?"
> He frowned quickly. "How did you know there was a letter?"
> She nodded her head in the boy's direction. "Big-Britches Jody
>   told me."
> Jody was embarrassed.

Question: How is the above incident organized?
Answer: Lines 5–8 report conversation between Jody's parents. Line 9 describes how someone was affected by that conversation: Jody was embarrassed.

Exercise 13.10: Writing About an Incident That Involves Conversation

Describe an incident that includes at least two or three sentences of real or imaginary conversation. In the final sentence, tell how someone was affected by that conversation.

Hints for Topics:

Someone congratulates you on your talk, report, idea, etc.
You ask a salesclerk in a store for help or information.
A classmate calls to invite you to a party.
A neighbor asks whether it is true that you are moving.
At a meeting, you make a motion that is defeated.
A friend asks about the health of someone in your family.
Someone unjustly rebukes you.
You overhear a conversation in which you are mentioned.

Just as I was leaving the building, a neighbor burdened with several packages was about to enter. "May I hold the door for you?" I asked, retracing my steps.

"Mind your own business! If I need any help, I'll ask for it."

I was shocked. "What did I do," I kept asking myself, "to deserve a remark like that?"

No one suggested a practical way for raising additional funds for the club's treasury. After a while, thinking that I had a sensible idea, I got up and said, "Madam President, I move that we raise the annual dues by two dollars."

"Does anyone here want to second that motion?" asked the president. Not a single hand went up. There was an embarrassing silence.

Finally, disappointed in my fellow members, I said, "Madam President, I withdraw my motion."

Now reread the directions and describe your incident.

_____

_____

_____

_____

_____

_____

_____

_____

_____

_____

_____

_____

_____

_____

_____

_____

_____

Gulliver's Travels

by Jonathan Swift

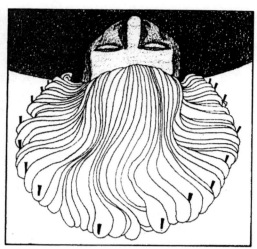

Gulliver, the only survivor of a shipwreck, is cast up on the shore of an unknown land, where a strange adventure befalls him.

I then advanced forward near half a mile, but could not discover any sign of houses or inhabitants; at least I was in so weak a condition, that I did not observe them. I was extremely tired, and with that, and the heat of the weather, and about half a pint
5 of brandy that I drank as I left the ship, I found myself much inclined to sleep. I lay down on the grass, which was very short and soft, where I slept sounder than ever I remember to have done in my life, and, as I reckoned, above nine hours; for when I awaked, it was just day-light. I attempted to rise, but was not able to stir:
10 for as I happened to lie on my back, I found my arms and legs were strongly fastened on each side to the ground; and my hair, which was long and thick, tied down in the same manner. I likewise felt several slender ligatures across my body, from my armpits to my thighs. I could only look upwards, the sun began to
15 grow hot, and the light offended my eyes. I heard a confused noise about me, but in the posture I lay, could see nothing except the sky. In a little time I felt something alive moving on my left leg, which advancing gently forward over my breast, came almost up to my chin; when bending my eyes downwards as much as I could,
20 I perceived it to be a human creature not six inches high, with a bow and arrow in his hands, and a quiver at his back. In the meantime, I felt at least forty more of the same kind (as I conjectured) following the first. I was in the utmost astonishment, and roared so loud, that they all ran back in a fright; and some of them, as I
25 was afterwards told, were hurt with the falls they got by leaping

from my sides upon the ground. However, they soon returned, and one of them, who ventured so far as to get a full sight of my face, lifting up his hands and eyes by way of admiration, cried out in a shrill, but distinct voice, *Hekinah degul:* the others repeated the
30 same words several times, but then I knew not what they meant. I lay all this while, as the reader may believe, in great uneasiness: at length, struggling to get loose, I had the fortune to break the strings, and wrench out the pegs that fastened my left arm to the ground; for, by lifting it up to my face, I discovered the methods
35 they had taken to bind me, and at the same time with a violent pull, which gave me excessive pain, I a little loosened the strings that tied down my hair on the left side, so that I was just able to turn my head about two inches.

Line 13. *ligatures:* strings

UNDERSTANDING THE SELECTION

Exercise 14.1: Close Reading

In the blank space, write the *letter* of the choice that best completes the statement or answers the question.

1. In the first half-mile or so of the narrator's walk from the shore, there __a__ .

   (A) were no houses or people
   (B) were people, but no houses
   (C) may have been houses and people

2. Which of the following—weariness, the weather, brandy—made the narrator sleepy? __C__

   (A) weariness and brandy
   (B) the weather and brandy
   (C) all three

3. When the narrator awoke, his main feeling was one of __B__ .

   (A) wonder
   (B) fear
   (C) weariness

4. The narrator is about __b__ times as tall as the people he is describing.

   (A) six
   (B) twelve
   (C) a hundred

5. The narrator was __B__ by the creature who first cried *Hekinah degul.*

    (A) hated
    (B) admired
    (C) attacked

6. How many creatures did the narrator see advancing over his body? __B__

    (A) none
    (B) at least forty
    (C) one or two

7. The selection does not reveal __B__ .

    (A) the means by which the narrator was tied
    (B) the meaning of *Hekinah degul*
    (C) the time at which the narrator awoke

8. The reader may infer that the narrator will __B__ .

    (A) be unable to free himself
    (B) learn the language of his captors
    (C) be swiftly expelled from the country

LEARNING NEW WORDS

Line	Word	Meaning	Typical Use
22	**conjecture** *(v.)* kən-'jek-chər	arrive at a conclusion through guesswork; guess; suppose	Since the lights were on, we *conjectured* that you were at home.
36	**excessive** *(adj.)* ik-'ses-iv	beyond what is usual, proper, or necessary; too great; extreme	People usually get rid of an old car when the cost of repair becomes *excessive.*
6	**inclined** *(adj.)* in-'klīnd	having an *inclination* (leaning) or tendency; disposed	Beginners are *inclined* to use excessive force in handling tools.
15	**offend** *(v.)* ə-'fend	cause pain to; hurt; displease	The music was so loud that it *offended* our ears.
29	**shrill** *(adj.)* 'shril	having a high-pitched sound; piercing	As the fire engines rushed to the scene, *shrill* sirens pierced the air.
31	**uneasiness** *(n.)* ˌən-'ē-zē-nəs	state of being uneasy (restless); feeling of worry; anxiety; disquiet	I was worried over your absence, and when I heard that you were in the hospital, my *uneasiness* increased.

23	**utmost** *(adj.)* 'ət-ˌmōst	greatest possible; of the greatest or highest degree	Since the roads were flooded, motorists were warned to drive with the *utmost* care.
27	**venture** *(v.)* 'ven-chər	proceed despite danger; dare to go; dare	Swimmers are warned not to *venture* beyond the patrolled area of the lake.
35	**violent** *(adj.)* 'vī-ə-lənt	acting or done with extreme force; fierce; furious	The marchers were peaceful, except for a small group of *vio- lent* individuals who tried to break through the police lines.
33	**wrench** *(v.)* 'rench	pull with a sudden twisting motion; twist violently	The wrestler twisted his oppo- nent's arm and nearly *wrenched* it from its socket.

APPLYING WHAT YOU HAVE LEARNED

Exercise 14.2: Sentence Completion

Which of the two choices correctly completes the sentence? Write the *letter* of your answer in the space provided.

1. The visitor was ＿＿＿ because you had offended him.

    A. kind   B. hurt

2. Excessive rain often causes ＿＿＿.

    A. flooding   B. storms

3. It was a violent meeting; ＿＿＿.

    A. there was standing room only   B. furniture was overturned

4. We are dealing with matters of the utmost danger. Ordinary safety measures ＿＿＿.

    A. must be followed   B. will not suffice

5. He wrenched the weapon from ＿＿＿.

    A. the ground   B. his attacker's grip

6. You would not expect a ＿＿＿ person to do much venturing.

    A. courageous   B. cowardly

7. Belle's uneasiness ＿＿＿.

    A. enabled her to solve the most   B. prevented her from getting enough
        difficult math problems   sleep

8. People inclined to giggle laugh more ____ than others.

A. easily   B. rarely

9. When you are ____, there is no need to conjecture.

A. in doubt   B. certain

10. Listening to a shrill voice can be very ____.

A. unpleasant   B. relaxing

Exercise 14.3: Definitions

Each expression below defines a word taught on pages 179–180. Enter that word in the space provided.

_____ **1.** acting with extreme force

_____ **2.** having a high-pitched sound

_____ **3.** proceed despite danger

_____ **4.** of the highest degree

_____ **5.** feeling of worry

_____ **6.** pull with a sudden twisting motion

_____ **7.** beyond what is proper or usual

_____ **8.** having a tendency

_____ **9.** cause pain to

_____ **10.** arrive at a conclusion through guesswork

Exercise 14.4: Synonyms and Antonyms

A. Replace each italicized word with a *synonym* from the vocabulary list below.

_____ **1.** I had to *twist* the bat from his grip.

_____ **2.** What is the reason for your *anxiety?*

_____ **3.** We'll defeat them if they *venture* to oppose us.

_____ **4.** At present Rhoda is not *disposed* to accept your apology.

_____ **5.** Have they done anything to *displease* you?

Vocabulary List

inclined	violent
conjectured	dare
excessive	utmost
wrench	offend
shrill	uneasiness

B. Replace each italicized expression with an *antonym* from the vocabulary list.

_____ 6. The Governor's arrival received the *least possible* publicity.

_____ 7. We *knew for a fact* that Sam had come back.

_____ 8. Mort has a *low-pitched* voice.

_____ 9. The amount of rainfall has been *below what is usual.*

_____ 10. Eileen's temper is *extremely gentle.*

LEARNING SOME ROOTS AND DERIVATIVES

Each word in bold type is a *root.* The words below it are its *derivatives.*

conjecture *(n.)*	A *conjecture* often turns out to be wrong.
conjecture *(v.)*	When we *conjecture,* we are guessing.
exceed *(v.)*	Your drapes should not *exceed* 90 inches in length.
excessive *(adj.)*	A length of more than 90 inches would be *excessive.*
excessively *(adv.)*	These drapes are *excessively* long.
excess *(n.)*	If you have too much material, what will you do with the *excess?*
incline *(v.)*	Some of us tend to side with the mayor; others *incline* toward the governor.
inclined *(adj.)*	Which way are you *inclined?*
inclination *(n.)*	What is your *inclination?*
offend *(v.)*	I did not wish to *offend* anyone.
offensive *(adj.)*	I did not wish to be *offensive.*
offensively *(adv.)*	If I have spoken *offensively,* I want to apologize.
offense *(n.)*	I intended no *offense* to anyone.
uneasy *(adj.)*	My sister is *uneasy* about her admission to college.
uneasily *(adv.)*	She is *uneasily* waiting to hear whether or not she has been accepted.
uneasiness *(n.)*	Her *uneasiness* is increasing.

utmost *(adj.)*	Your request will receive our *utmost* attention and consideration.
utmost *(n.)*	We shall do our *utmost* to help.
venture *(v.)*	Some of the unemployed engineers have decided to *venture* into a new field.
venture *(n.)*	They are inclined to leave engineering to embark on a new *venture*.
venturesome *(adj.)*	Others are not so *venturesome*.
violent *(adj.)*	The argument grew *violent*.
violently *(adv.)*	Both sides *violently* disagreed.
violence *(n.)*	The meeting had to be adjourned because of the *violence* of the argument.
wrench *(v.)*	I tried to *wrench* my arm free.
wrench *(n.)*	I tried to free my arm with a sudden *wrench*.

Exercise 14.5: Roots and Derivatives

Fill each blank with the root or derivative just listed that best completes the sentence.

1. After completing one daring mission, the special agent undertook an even more dangerous _____ .

2. The police were afraid a fight would develop, but fortunately there was no _____ .

3. Before coming to this class I was lazy and had little _____ for work.

4. I know I am not to blame, and I will do my _____ to prove it.

5. What I have told you is not a(n) _____ but a fact.

6. Realizing that she might be late for the interview, Helen began to feel _____ .

7. Instead of releasing my arm, he gave it a(n) _____ that made me scream.

8. If you have more equipment than you need, send the _____ back to the supply room.

9. Phil is quite daring, but his cousin is not so _____ .

10. Forgive me if my remark displeased you. I did not intend it as a(n) _____ .

Exercise 14.6: Defining Roots and Derivatives

Enter the word from pages 182–183 that matches the definition below.

1. fiercely; furiously   _____

2. go beyond a set limit; surpass   _____

3. tendency; leaning   _____

4. restlessly; anxiously   _____

5. displeasingly; in a manner to cause pain   _____

6. guess; suppose   _____

7. lean; tend   _____

8. extremely; in a manner beyond what is usual   _____

9. irritating; displeasing   _____

10. the part beyond what is necessary; surplus   _____

IMPROVING YOUR SPELLING: *IE* AND *EI*

In some words, the sound of ē as in the word *ēve* is spelled *ie:*

"I lay all this while, as the reader may bel*ie*ve, in great uneasiness . . ."

In certain other words, the very same sound is spelled *ei:*

". . . I perc*ei*ved it to be a human creature not six inches high . . ."

How can you tell whether to use IE or EI in a particular word? To solve this problem, learn the following:

1. *Write* I *before* E:

ach*ie*ve	ch*ie*f	p*ie*ce	s*ie*ge
bel*ie*ve	f*ie*rce	rel*ie*ve	y*ie*ld, etc.

   Except after C:

c*ei*ling	conc*ei*ve	dec*ei*ve	rec*ei*pt
conc*ei*t	dec*ei*t	perc*ei*ve	rec*ei*ve, etc.

2. Give special attention to five more exceptions, all of which have E before I:

   *ei*ther   n*ei*ther   l*ei*sure   s*ei*ze   w*ei*rd

Exercise 14.7: *IE* or *EI?*
Insert the missing letters and write the complete word.

	Column A	*Column B*
1.	gr __ __ f	_____
2.	f __ __ rceness	_____
3.	inconc __ __ vable	_____
4.	shr __ __ k	_____
5.	n __ __ ther	_____
6.	rel __ __ f	_____
7.	s __ __ zure	_____
8.	ch __ __ ftain	_____
9.	bes __ __ ged	_____
10.	dec __ __ tful	_____
11.	p __ __ rcing	_____
12.	th __ __ f	_____
13.	__ __ ther	_____
14.	n __ __ ce	_____
15.	l __ __ surely	_____
16.	unbel __ __ vable	_____
17.	rec __ __ ver	_____
18.	ach __ __ vement	_____
19.	w __ __ rd	_____
20.	c __ __ ling	_____
21.	bel __ __ f	_____
22.	y __ __ lding	_____
23.	conc __ __ ted	_____
24.	rec __ __ pt	_____
25.	bel __ __ ver	_____

Which, who, and *that* are pronouns that *relate* back to a previous word. Therefore, we call them **relative pronouns.**

Jonathan Swift wrote:

"I lay down on the grass, *which* was very short and soft . . ."

In the above sentence, *which* is a relative pronoun because it relates back to the noun *grass.*

The word to which a relative pronoun relates, or refers, is called its **antecedent.** In the above sentence, *grass* is the antecedent of the relative pronoun *which.*

Note the following:

1. You may use *which* if its antecedent is a thing.

   . . . my hair, *which* was long and thick . . .

2. You may use *who* if its antecedent is a person.

   . . . one of them, *who* ventured so far as to get a full sight of my face . . .

3. You may use *that* if its antecedent is either a thing or a person.

   This is the bus *that* goes downtown.
   I know a man *that* can speak four languages.

Exercise 14.8: Relative Pronoun and Antecedent
Underline the relative pronoun once and the antecedent twice. Example:

I just finished reading <u>Shane</u>, <u>which</u> I enjoyed very much.

1. Where is the girl that was just here?
2. We were waiting for some friends who had promised to meet us after school.
3. This is the problem which has been giving me trouble.
4. The players who were chosen are Mike, Allen, Barry, and I.
5. There is the mosquito that has been annoying me.

Exercise 14.9: Using Relative Pronouns
Enter the correct choice.

1. Name all the English teachers _____ you have already had. (*that* or *which*)
2. On his left leg, Gulliver felt something moving, _____ crept up to his chin. (*which* or *who*)

3. Are these the workers _____ were here last week? *(that* or *which)*

4. After the rain I saw some worms _____ had come up from the soil. *(who* or *that)*

5. Will you get in touch with the members _____ were absent from the meeting?

   (which or *who)*

IMPROVING YOUR COMPOSITION SKILLS: DESCRIBING A DIFFICULT SITUATION

On awakening, the narrator of *Gulliver's Travels* finds himself in a difficult situation—he is firmly fastened to the ground, he has no freedom of movement, and he can see nothing but the sky (pages 177–178).

Exercise 14.10: Account of a Difficult Situation

In a paragraph of about a hundred words, describe a difficult situation—real or imaginary—in which your freedom of movement or use of your senses was temporarily restricted.

If you wish, you may organize the paragraph as follows:

FIRST SENTENCE OR TWO: Explain how you got into the difficult situation.
NEXT THREE OR FOUR SENTENCES: Describe how your freedom was restricted.
LAST SENTENCE OR TWO: Explain how you got out of the difficult situation.

Hints for Topics:

You are caught in a slow moving crowd.
You are a passenger in a congested bus, train, or car.
You have a heavy cast on a broken arm or leg.
You are in a narrow, uncomfortable seat.
You are stalled on a long, slow-moving checkout line.

Sample Paragraph

> Last Saturday, my cousin arrived in her shiny red car and insisted on taking us to lunch. My sister sat up front with her, and my brothers and I squeezed into the back seat, with me in the middle. There was very little headroom and almost no legroom. It was even hard for me to move my arms. I was so cramped that I could scarcely breathe. Fortunately, it was just a five-minute ride to the pizza shop, but when I unbuckled my seat belt and got out of the car, I was thankful that I could stretch my arms and legs and breathe again.

Now write your paragraph.

_____

_____

_____

_____

_____

_____

_____

_____

_____

_____

_____

_____

_____

_____

_____

Rip Van Winkle

by Washington Irving

*What sort of person was Rip Van Winkle before he wandered into the Cats-
kills, where he fell asleep and slept for twenty years?*

Certain it is that he was a great favorite among all the good wives
of the village, who, as usual with the amiable sex, took his part
in all family squabbles; and never failed, whenever they talked
those matters over in their evening gossipings, to lay all the blame
on Dame Van Winkle. The children of the village, too, would shout
with joy whenever he approached. He assisted at their sports,
made their playthings, taught them to fly kites and shoot marbles,
and told them long stories of ghosts, witches, and Indians. Whenever he went dodging about the village, he was surrounded by a
troop of them hanging on his skirts, clambering on his back, and
playing a thousand tricks on him with impunity; and not a dog
would bark at him throughout the neighborhood.

The great error in Rip's composition was an insuperable aversion to all kinds of profitable labor. It could not be from the want
of assiduity or perseverance; for he would sit on a wet rock, with
a rod as long and heavy as a Tartar's lance, and fish all day
without a murmur, even though he should not be encouraged by
a single nibble. He would carry a fowling-piece on his shoulder for
hours together, trudging through woods and swamps, and up hill
and down dale, to shoot a few squirrels or wild pigeons. He would
never refuse to assist a neighbor even in the roughest toil, and
was a foremost man at all country frolics for husking Indian corn,
or building stone fences; the women of the village, too, used to
employ him to run their errands, and to do such little odd jobs as
their less obliging husbands would not do for them. In a word, Rip

was ready to attend to anybody's business but his own; but as to doing family duty, and keeping his farm in order, he found it impossible.

In fact, he declared it was of no use to work on his farm; it was
30 the most pestilent little piece of ground in the whole country; everything about it went wrong, and would go wrong, in spite of him. His fences were continually falling to pieces; his cow would either go astray, or get among the cabbages; weeds were sure to grow quicker in his fields than anywhere else; the rain always
35 made a point of setting in just as he had some outdoor work to do; so that though his patrimonial estate had dwindled away under his management, acre by acre, until there was little more left than a mere patch of Indian corn and potatoes, yet it was the worst conditioned farm in the neighborhood.

Line 13. *insuperable:* not able to be overcome

Line 15. *assiduity:* close attention

Line 30. *pestilent:* annoying

Line 36. *patrimonial:* inherited

UNDERSTANDING THE SELECTION

Exercise 15.1: Close Reading

In the blank space, write the *letter* of the choice that best completes the statement.

1. The women of the village _____.

   (A) got no help from their husbands
   (B) were remarkably alike in their opinions
   (C) liked Dame Van Winkle better than Rip

2. Rip was not on excellent terms with _____.

   (A) his neighbors
   (B) the children of the village
   (C) his wife

3. The children of the village _____.

   (A) took advantage of Rip's good nature
   (B) were not interested in Rip's long stories
   (C) did not like Rip's interfering with their games

4. Rip was especially good at _____.

   (A) running errands
   (B) country frolics
   (C) doing odd jobs

5. Rip ____ .

    (A) was never around when there was hard work to be done
    (B) had lost most of his property
    (C) would drop any undertaking at the slightest discouragement

6. The author finds something to criticize in ____ of the village.

    (A) the men but not the women
    (B) the women but not the men
    (C) both the men and the women

7. The reader learns relatively little about ____ .

    (A) Dame Van Winkle
    (B) Rip's farm
    (C) the children of the village

8. The author's main purpose seems to be to ____ .

    (A) furnish the reader with some worthy examples to follow
    (B) condemn harshly every instance of ignorance and stupidity
    (C) amuse and entertain the reader

LEARNING NEW WORDS

Line	Word	Meaning	Typical Use
36	**dwindle** (v.) 'dwin-d'l	become less; waste away; decrease (*ant.* **increase**)	The town's population, once more than 4,000, has *dwindled* to 982.
1	**favorite** (n.) 'fāv-ə-rət	person or thing *favored* (preferred) above others, or regarded with special liking; contestant regarded as most likely to win	Of his three daughters, the King especially liked the youngest; she was his *favorite*.
22	**foremost** (adj.) 'fȯr-‚mōst	first in rank; most important; leading (*ant.* **last**)	With an area of 586,400 square miles, Alaska is *foremost* among the states of the Union in size.
22	**frolic** (n.) 'fräl-ik	merry game or party; occasion of fun, gaiety, or merriment	Our school's field day promises to be a very enjoyable *frolic*.

4	**gossip** (v.) 'gäs-əp	indulge in idle talk or rumors about others; repeat what one knows about other people and their affairs	Some people love to *gossip* about the private affairs of others with anyone who will listen.
11	**impunity** (n.) im-'pyü-nət-ē	freedom from punishment or other bad consequences	Speeders risk heavy fines, loss of license, or serious injury; they cannot continue to break the law with *impunity*.
38	**mere** (adj.) 'miər	nothing more than; simple	My injury was not serious; it was a *mere* scratch.
25	**obliging** (adj.) ə-'blī-jiŋ	willing to *oblige* (do favors); accommodating; helpful; cooperative	The salesclerk offered to gift-wrap the present; she was very *obliging*.
		(*ant.* **disobliging**)	If Ann were to ask her brother for a favor, he might turn her down; he can be quite *disobliging*.
		(*ant.* **inconsiderate**)	It is *inconsiderate* to make one call after another when others are waiting to use the telephone.
15	**perseverance** (n.) ‚pər-sə-'vir-əns	action of sticking to a purpose despite difficulties; steadfastness; persistence	If you give up easily after one or two failures, you lack *perseverance*.
3	**squabble** (n.) 'skwäb-əl	noisy quarrel, usually over a trifle; bickering	The game was interrupted by a *squabble* over whether the ball I had hit was fair or foul.

APPLYING WHAT YOU HAVE LEARNED

Exercise 15.2: Sentence Completion

Which of the two choices correctly completes the sentence? Write the *letter* of your answer in the space provided.

1. Steve _____ his lawn mower; he has perseverance.

   A. keeps trying to repair   B. is getting rid of

2. The obliging stranger moved to another seat so that _____.

   A. he could have a better view   B. my friend and I could sit together
      of the screen

3. Our neighbors are having another squabble; they are always ____.

    A. quarreling   B. giving parties

4. ____ whatever you learn about the neighbors; do not gossip.

    A. Keep to yourself   B. Share with others

5. Strawberry ice cream must be your favorite, since you ____ ask for another flavor.

    A. frequently   B. seldom

6. I wouldn't agree that Cliff is the foremost storyteller in our class, but I would say that he is ____.

    A. second to none   B. one of the best

7. Come to our frolic for an evening of ____.

    A. fun and merriment   B. peace and quiet

8. If I had managed the family savings, they would have dwindled by now to ____.

    A. a respectable fortune   B. almost nothing

9. May I hand in the report late with impunity, or will there be ____ penalty?

    A. no   B. some

10. I felt that I ____ because I was dealing with a mere child.

    A. could relax   B. had to be on my guard

Exercise 15.3: Definitions

Each expression below defines a word taught on pages 191–192. Enter that word in the space provided.

_____   **1.** first in rank

_____   **2.** freedom from bad consequences

_____   **3.** noisy quarrel

_____   **4.** become less

_____   **5.** willing to do favors

_____   **6.** merry game or party

_____   **7.** nothing more than

_____   **8.** person regarded with special liking

_____   **9.** repeat what one knows about others

_____   **10.** action of sticking to a purpose despite difficulties

Exercise 15.4: Synonyms and Antonyms

Fill the blanks with the required synonyms or antonyms, selecting them from the vocabulary list below.

1. synonym for *persistence*   _____
2. antonym for *inconsiderate*   _____
3. synonym for *party*   _____
4. synonym for *bickering*   _____
5. antonym for *last*   _____
6. synonym for *repeat rumors*   _____
7. synonym for *simple*   _____
8. synonym for *preferred person*   _____
9. antonym for *increase*   _____
10. synonym for *freedom from punishment* _____

Vocabulary List

frolic	dwindle
mere	obliging
foremost	gossip
impunity	squabble
perseverance	favorite

LEARNING SOME ROOTS AND DERIVATIVES

Each word in bold type is a **root**. The words below it are its **derivatives**.

favor *(v.)*   My grandparents *favor* my baby sister.

favorite *(adj.)*   She is their *favorite* grandchild.

favorite *(n.)*   She is their *favorite*.

frolic *(v.)*   The children love to *frolic* on the beach.

frolic *(n.)*   Will you join them in their *frolic?*

gossip *(v.)*   The neighbors gathered to *gossip*.

gossip *(n.)*   Have you heard the latest *gossip?*

mere *(adj.)*   I was a *mere* beginner.

merely *(adv.)*   I was *merely* a beginner.

Vocabulary and Composition Through Pleasurable Reading, Book I

oblige *(v.)*	The management was glad to *oblige* me.
obliging *(adj.)*	It was very *obliging*.
obligingly *(adv.)*	*Obligingly*, it gave me a refund.
persevere *(v.)*	You may reach your goal if you *persevere*.
persevering *(adj.)*	Be *persevering!*
perseveringly *(adv.)*	Pursue your goal *perseveringly!*
perseverance *(n.)*	By *perseverance*, you will get ahead.
squabble *(n.)*	I don't want to get into another *squabble*.
squabble *(v.)*	Let's not *squabble* anymore about who was at fault.

Exercise 15.5: Roots and Derivatives

From the words listed on pages 194–195, select the best synonym for the word or words in parentheses.

1. A sad occasion is no time to *(make merry)* _____.

2. If you *(remain steadfast in spite of difficulties)* _____, you may yet win out.

3. Whom do you *(prefer)* _____ for captain, Janet or Louise?

4. It is silly to *(quarrel noisily)* _____.

5. Will you *(do a favor for)* _____ me by allowing me to use your pen?

6. The detectives assigned to the case followed up each clue *(in a persistent manner)* _____.

7. Who is your *(best-liked)* _____ movie star?

8. Would you be so *(cooperative)* _____ as to hold my books while I tie my shoe?

9. Let us not be swayed by *(idle talk)* _____.

10. It was not much of a rain, *(simply)* _____ a sunshower.

IMPROVING YOUR SPELLING: FORMING THE PLURAL OF NOUNS ENDING IN -O

Rip raised Indian corn and *potatoes*.
In Rip's time there were no *radios*.

From the preceding we can see that some words ending in -O, like *potato,* add -*ES* to form the plural:

> potato + es = potato*es*

Some words, however, like *radio,* merely add -*S*:

> radio + s = radio*s*

To know when to add -S and when to attach -ES, study the following:

1. Add -S if the noun ends in -O preceded by a *vowel.*

> radio—radio*s*   rodeo—rodeo*s*   ratio—ratio*s,* etc.

2. If the noun ends in -O preceded by a *consonant,* the situation is as follows:

   a. Some nouns add -ES.

   > potato—potatoes   mosquito—mosquitoes   torpedo—torpedoes
   > tomato—tomatoes   echo—echoes   veto—vetoes
   > hero—heroes   embargo—embargoes

   b. Some nouns add -S.

   > auto—autos   piano—pianos   soprano—sopranos   solo—solos

   c. Some nouns add either -ES or -S.

   > cargo—cargoes or cargos   tornado—tornadoes or tornados
   > motto—mottoes or mottos   volcano—volcanoes or volcanos
   > buffalo—buffaloes or buffalos   zero—zeroes or zeros
   > domino—dominoes or dominos

Exercise 15.6: Forming Plurals

Write the plural of the nouns below. Included among them are nouns that we have previously studied. If necessary, review page 128.

1. studio _____
2. tomato _____
3. glass _____
4. woman _____
5. fox _____
6. ox _____
7. hero _____
8. child _____
9. fly _____
10. mosquito _____

11. auto _____
12. bench _____
13. portfolio _____
14. turkey _____
15. rodeo _____
16. lady _____
17. piano _____
18. potato _____
19. highway _____
20. folio _____

Here are five pairs of verbs frequently misused:

1. Learn and teach

To *learn* means "to receive knowledge."

> From Rip, the children *learned* to fly kites.

To *teach* means "to show" or "instruct."

> Rip *taught* (not *learned*) the children to fly kites.

2. Borrow and lend

To *borrow* means "to take something from someone temporarily with the understanding that it must be returned."

> May I *borrow* (not *lend*) your eraser?

To *lend* means "to let another person use something temporarily with the understanding that it must be returned."

> I shall be glad to *lend* you the money.

3. Bring and take

To *bring* means "to carry toward" the speaker.

> Please *bring* the photographs the next time you come.

To *take* means "to carry away from" the speaker.

> *Take* (not *Bring*) these letters to the post office.

4. Leave and let

To *leave* means (1) "to depart," or (2) "to let remain."

> When you *leave,* turn off the lights.
> *Leave* the door open.

To *let* means "to permit" or "allow."

> *Let* (not *Leave*) her have a chance to speak.

5. Can and may

Can is a helping verb expressing ability.

> *Can* you (Are you able to) skate?

May is a helping verb expressing (1) permission, or (2) possibility.

> *May* (not *Can*) I borrow your notes?
> It *may* snow tonight.

Exercise 15.7: Using the Right Verb

1. I _____ a quarter from Maureen. *(borrowed* or *lent)*

2. _____ I please have the sugar? *(May* or *Can)*

3. Do not take the milk out; _____ it in the refrigerator. *(let* or *leave)*

4. Uncle Ben _____ me to play the guitar. *(learned* or *taught)*

5. _____ him solve his own problems. *(Let* or *Leave)*

6. Ms. Jones asked me to _____ the attendance report to the office. *(bring* or *take)*

7. You can't _____ an old dog new tricks. *(teach* or *learn)*

8. Tell the neighbor's boy that we have just enough sugar for dinner and that we can't _____ any. *(borrow* or *lend)*

9. Why not _____ your friend to our next meeting? *(bring* or *take)*

10. You _____ have as much time as you need. *(may* or *can)*

IMPROVING YOUR COMPOSITION SKILLS: SUPPORTING A GENERAL STATEMENT

When Washington Irving makes a general statement, he immediately supports that statement with reasons, examples, and specific details. Here is a sample from page 189, lines 5–6:

General Statement:

The children of the village, too, would shout with joy whenever he approached.

Irving follows with two sentences of supporting material. Both give *reasons* for the children's shouts of joy at Rip's approach. They also give *examples* and *specific details* of what Rip did for the children—and what they did to him.

Supporting Material:

He assisted at their sports, made their playthings, taught them to fly kites and shoot marbles, and told them long stories of ghosts, witches, and Indians. Whenever he went dodging about the village, he was surrounded by a troop of them hanging on his skirts, clambering on his back, and playing a thousand tricks on him with impunity.

Exercise 15.8: Using Reasons, Examples, and Specific Details

In a paragraph of about four or five sentences, support a general statement with reasons, examples, and specific details.

You may begin with one of the following general statements or with one of your own:

Spring (or some other time) is my favorite season.
I am nervous when I ride with an inexperienced driver.
Basketball (or some other sport) is exciting to watch.
Something is always breaking down in our house (or building).
When I am in a hurry, I tend to be careless.
We have had a successful (or disappointing) year.
Things have improved (or worsened) since the new management took over.

Sample Paragraph

> Something is always breaking down in our building. Last winter, when the boiler burst, we were without heat and hot water for four days. A short time later, after a heavy snow, the roof began to leak, and it still leaks when it rains because it has not been properly repaired. The leaks are so bad that tenants in the upper-floor apartments are afraid their ceilings will collapse. And today, for the second time this week, the elevator is not running.

Now write your paragraph.

_____

_____

_____

_____

_____

_____

_____

_____

_____

_____

_____

_____

_____

_____

The Story of My Life

by Helen Keller

At the age of nineteen months, Helen Keller was stricken by an illness that destroyed her ability to hear, speak, and see. Nevertheless she became one of the most famous persons of the twentieth century.

But what was she like as a child—angel or devil?

About this time I found out the use of a key. One morning I locked my mother up in the pantry, where she was obliged to remain three hours, as the servants were in a detached part of the house. She kept pounding on the door, while I sat outside on the porch
5 steps and laughed with glee as I felt the jar of the pounding. This most naughty prank of mine convinced my parents that I must be taught as soon as possible. After my teacher, Miss Sullivan, came to me, I sought an early opportunity to lock her in her room. I went upstairs with something which my mother made me under-
10 stand I was to give to Miss Sullivan; but no sooner had I given it to her than I slammed the door to, locked it, and hid the key under the wardrobe in the hall. I could not be induced to tell where the key was. My father was obliged to get a ladder and take Miss Sullivan out through the window—much to my delight. Months after
15 I produced the key.

When I was about five years old we moved from the little vine-covered house to a large new one. The family consisted of my father and mother, two older half-brothers, and, afterward, a little sister, Mildred. My earliest distinct recollection of my father is
20 making my way through great drifts of newspapers to his side and finding him alone, holding a sheet of paper before his face. I was greatly puzzled to know what he was doing. I imitated this action, even wearing his spectacles, thinking they might help solve the

mystery. But I did not find out the secret for several years. Then
25 I learned what those papers were, and that my father edited one
of them.

My father was most loving and indulgent, devoted to his home,
seldom leaving us, except in the hunting season. He was a great
hunter, I have been told, and a celebrated shot. Next to his family
30 he loved his dogs and gun. His hospitality was great, almost to a
fault, and he seldom came home without bringing a guest.

UNDERSTANDING THE SELECTION

Exercise 16.1: Close Reading

In the blank space, write the *letter* of the choice that best completes the statement.

1. After Helen locked her mother in the pantry, her parents _____.

   (A) did not allow her to play with keys
   (B) became concerned about her education
   (C) punished her

2. Miss Sullivan was locked in her room _____.

   (A) as the result of a carefully laid plan
   (B) for three hours
   (C) accidentally

3. The selection indicates that _____.

   (A) Miss Sullivan was a strict teacher
   (B) the Keller family was poor
   (C) Helen was mischievous

4. Helen learned about her father's skill as a hunter _____.

   (A) from her father himself
   (B) by accompanying him on hunting trips
   (C) from others

5. As a child, Helen was _____.

   (A) unwilling to learn
   (B) curious
   (C) lazy

6. Helen was _____ in a family of four children.

   (A) next to the youngest
   (B) the oldest
   (C) the youngest

7. Helen's sense of _____ told her that her mother was pounding on a door.

   (A) hearing
   (B) sight
   (C) touch

8. Miss Sullivan's room could have been _____ .

   (A) locked if the door had accidentally slammed shut
   (B) unlocked without a key from the inside only
   (C) unlocked from the inside or outside with a key only

LEARNING NEW WORDS

Line	Word	Meaning	Typical Use
6	**convince** (v.) kən-'vins	persuade by proof; make feel sure; overcome the doubts of	We have learned enough to con-*vince* us that smoking is harmful to health.
19	**distinct** (adj.) dis-'tiŋkt	clearly seen or heard; plain; unmistakable	It is easy to understand someone whose speech is *distinct*.
		(ant. **indistinct, vague**)	Your note, "Will be back soon," was too *vague*. We could not tell when you would return.
5	**glee** (n.) 'glē	lively joy; mirth; delight; hilarity	The children shouted with *glee* when they heard they were going to the swimming pool.
		(ant. **gloom**)	They had every reason to be joyful and happy. There was no cause for *gloom*.
31	**guest** (n.) 'gest	person entertained at the home of another (known as the *host*); visitor	When you come to my house, you are my *guest* and I am your host.
22	**imitate** (v.) 'im-ə-ˌtāt	copy; follow as a model or example	A baby learns to speak by *imitating* its parents.
12	**induce** (v.) in-'dyüs	lead on to do something; influence; persuade	The purpose of a TV or radio commercial is to *induce* us to buy something.
27	**indulgent** (adj.) in-'dəlj-ənt	excessively kind; lenient	Whom would you rather have—a strict teacher or an *indulgent* one?
		(ant. **strict**)	

4	**pound** (v.)	strike with heavy blows again and again; hit hard repeatedly; beat	Don't *pound* on the door; knock gently.
	'pau̇nd		
6	**prank** (n.)	playful or mischievous act; practical joke; trick	Did you lose your books, or has someone hidden them as a *prank?*
	'praŋk		
19	**recollection** (n.)	power of recalling to mind; memory; remembrance	Do you have a clear *recollection* of your first haircut, or have you forgotten?
	ˌrek-ə-'lek-shən		

APPLYING WHAT YOU HAVE LEARNED

Exercise 16.2: Sentence Completion

Which of the two choices correctly completes the sentence? Write the *letter* of your answer in the space provided.

1. A _____ occasion is no time for glee.

   A. sad   B. happy

2. My recollection is not too good. How _____?

   A. good is your handwriting   B. is your memory

3. When I visit you next month, _____ guest.

   A. I will be your   B. you will be my

4. Do you _____, or are you convinced?

   A. feel sure   B. have some doubt

5. When informed she had won, Blanche suspected a prank, but it turned out to be _____.

   A. a trick   B. the truth

6. The champion pounded his opponent, landing several _____ blows.

   A. light   B. heavy

7. My uncle is indulgent; he always _____ his children when they do something wrong.

   A. forgives   B. punishes

8. Your directions were so distinct that we _____.

   A. easily found the place   B. lost our way

9. No one induced me to drop out of the election; ____.

    A. it was my own decision   B. my friends said I couldn't win

10. Paul does not imitate others; he ____ ideas.

    A. borrows his   B. creates his own

Exercise 16.3: Definitions

Each expression below defines a word taught on pages 202–203. Enter that word in the space provided.

_____ **1.** follow as an example

_____ **2.** mischievous act

_____ **3.** lead on to do something

_____ **4.** person entertained by a host

_____ **5.** persuade by proof

_____ **6.** hit hard repeatedly

_____ **7.** clearly seen or heard

_____ **8.** power of recalling to mind

_____ **9.** excessively kind

_____ **10.** lively joy

Exercise 16.4: Synonyms and Antonyms

Fill the blanks with the required synonyms or antonyms, selecting them from the words taught on pages 202–203.

1. synonym for *copy*   _____

2. antonym for *strict*   _____

3. synonym for *trick*   _____

4. synonym for *remembrance*   _____

5. synonym for *beat*   _____

6. antonym for *vague*   _____

7. synonym for *overcome the doubts of*   _____

8. antonym for *gloom*   _____

9. synonym for *visitor*   _____

10. synonym for *influence*   _____

LEARNING SOME ROOTS AND DERIVATIVES

Each word in bold type is a *root.* The words below it are its *derivatives.*

convince *(v.)*   You should be able to *convince* others.

convincing *(adj.)*   Your evidence is *convincing.*

convincingly *(adv.)*   You argue *convincingly.*

conviction *(n.)*   You speak with *conviction.*

distinguish *(v.)*   It is easy to *distinguish* every student in this excellent group photograph.

distinct *(adj.)*   Everyone's face is *distinct.*

distinctly *(adv.)*   Everybody's features are *distinctly* visible.

distinctness *(n.)*   Everyone can be seen with *distinctness.*

glee *(n.)*   The guests were full of *glee.*

gleeful *(adj.)*   They were especially *gleeful* when the cake was brought in.

gleefully *(adv.)*   They applauded *gleefully* when I blew out the candles.

imitate *(v.)*   This is my own work. I did not *imitate* anybody.

imitator *(n.)*   I am not an *imitator.*

imitation *(n.)*   This is original work, not an *imitation.*

induce *(v.)*   Mother can *induce* Billy to wash his face by offering him a cookie.

inducement *(n.)*   Mother uses cookies as an *inducement* with Billy.

indulge *(v.)*   Some parents *indulge* their children too much.

indulgent *(adj.)*   Such parents are excessively *indulgent.*

indulgently *(adv.)*   They raise their children *indulgently.*

indulgence *(n.)*   They shower them with *indulgence.*

prank *(n.)*   Billy loves to play a *prank.*

prankish *(adj.)*   He is a *prankish* child.

prankishly *(adv.)*   He will come up to you and say, *prankishly:* "Close your eyes."

recollect *(v.)*   I do not *recollect* promising you anything.

recollection *(n.)*   I have no *recollection* of promising you anything.

Exercise 16.5: Roots and Derivatives

Fill each blank below with the root or derivative just listed that best completes the sentence.

1. As soon as the contest ended, the winning team ran _____ from the field.

2. I searched my memory but could not _____ where I had seen her before.

3. On a clear night it is easy to _____ the North Star.

4. Some parents believe that strictness is better than _____ in bringing up their children.

5. If you look up when you speak, instead of at your notes, we will be able to hear you more _____.

6. Because your reasons were so _____, I felt sure that your answer was correct.

7. Do you create designs of your own, or are you merely a(n) _____.

8. As a(n) _____ for customers to come to its grand opening, the new store is offering free gifts.

9. Watch out for my _____ cousin; he likes to play practical jokes.

10. Is this real leather, or just a(an) _____?

Exercise 16.6: Defining Roots and Derivatives

Enter the word from page 205 that matches the definition below.

1. in an excessively kind way   _____

2. merry; full of mirth   _____

3. feeling of being right beyond any doubt   _____

4. make out; see or hear clearly   _____

5. in a mischievous manner   _____

6. be very lenient with; give way to   _____

7. clearness; definiteness   _____

8. something that leads one on to do something   _____

9. recall to mind; remember   _____

10. in a way that overcomes doubts   _____

IMPROVING YOUR SPELLING: ADDING THE SUFFIXES -OR AND -ER

The suffixes **-or** and **-er** have the same meaning: "one who."

imitate + or (one who) = imitator (one who imitates)

observe + er (one who) = observer (one who observes)

But how can we tell whether a noun ends in **-or** (as in *imitator*) or **-er** (as in *observer*)?

1. If you can trace the noun to a verb of at least two syllables ending in *ate,* use **-or** with that noun. For example:

imit*ATE*	imitat*OR*
cre*ATE*	creat*OR*
demonstr*ATE*	demonstrat*OR*
investig*ATE*	investigat*OR*

Exception: deb*ate*—deb*ate*r

2. Aside from the above clue, there is no easy way to tell whether a noun ends in **-or** or **-er.** You will have to study each of the most frequently used *-or* and *-er* nouns. Consult your dictionary whenever necessary. Here are some words to review:

-OR		-ER	
ambassador	mayor	buyer	owner
author	monitor	defender	pleader
contributor	possessor	interpreter	pretender
creditor	professor	invader	printer
debtor	senator	laborer	purchaser
governor	supervisor	manufacturer	reporter
janitor	tailor	offender	supporter
juror		organizer	

3. Study these few nouns ending in **-ar:**

beggar burglar liar scholar

Exercise 16.7: Changing Verbs to Nouns

Change each verb below to a noun by adding -OR, -ER, or -AR.

1. own: _____
2. regulate: _____
3. pretend: _____
4. beg: _____
5. contribute: _____
6. narrate: _____
7. support: _____
8. create: _____
9. labor: _____
10. defend: _____

11. indicate: _____
12. buy: _____
13. elevate: _____
14. offend: _____
15. govern: _____
16. plead: _____
17. debate: _____
18. translate: _____
19. manufacture: _____
20. navigate: _____

Exercise 16.8: Using the Right Suffix

Add -OR, -ER, or -AR to the words in the first column and write the complete word in the second column.

1. janit_____   _____
2. burgl_____   _____
3. ambassad_____   _____
4. organiz_____   _____
5. schol_____   _____
6. may_____   _____
7. report_____   _____
8. senat_____   _____
9. tail_____   _____
10. invad_____   _____

USING APPOSITIVES

1. An **appositive** is a noun or phrase placed right next to another noun and giving additional information about that noun.

"After my teacher, *Miss Sullivan,* came to me, I sought an early opportunity to lock her in her room."

Note here that the noun *Miss Sullivan* is an appositive; it is placed right next to the noun *teacher,* and it gives additional information about that noun.

In the following sentence, the phrase *the capital of New York State* is an appositive:

Albany, *the capital of New York State,* is on the Hudson River.

2. An appositive is set off from the rest of the sentence by commas.

WITHIN THE SENTENCE—2 COMMAS

Archie Molloy (,) <u>a fast eater</u> (,) was the first to finish.
appositive

BEGINNING OF THE SENTENCE—1 COMMA

<u>A fast eater</u> (,) Archie Molloy was the first to finish.
appositive

END OF THE SENTENCE—1 COMMA

The first to finish was Archie Molloy (,) <u>a fast eater</u>.
appositive

3. No commas are used when the appositive is so closely associated with the noun it explains that the two are pronounced with no pause between them.

My brother *Jack* waited for me.
William *the Conqueror* invaded England in 1066.
The word *sheriff* has one *r* and two *f*'s.

Exercise 16.9: Punctuating Sentences Containing Appositives
Rewrite each sentence, inserting all necessary punctuation.

1. Skippy our neighbor's dog barks at strangers

_____

2. I went to Room 209 the Dean's Office

_____

3. Alexander the Great died at the age of 33

_____

4. The cactus a desert plant has beautiful flowers

_____

5. Didn't my cousin Jim tell you I was ill

_____

Exercise 16.10: Conciseness
By using an appositive, combine each pair of sentences below into a single sentence.

SAMPLE: Larry rides a motorbike. He is the boy with the red hair.
Larry, the boy with the red hair, rides a motorbike.

1. Henry hurt his knee. He is our best pitcher.

_____

2. George Orwell wrote *Animal Farm.* It is a fascinating novel.

_____

3. Helen Keller was a mischievous child. She was full of pranks.

_____

4. The next course was corned beef and cabbage. It was the main dish.

_____

5. Martin Luther King influenced millions of Americans. He was a gifted leader.

_____

6. Next week we will play the Lions. They are an undefeated team.

_____

7. Tabby brushed against my leg. She is my friend's cat.

_____

8. In New Hampshire I climbed to the top of Mt. Washington. It is the highest mountain in the East.

_____

9. Abby will play either "Rhapsody in Blue" or "Autumn Leaves." They are her favorite piano pieces.

_____

10. Karate is a system of self-defense without weapons. Many people are studying it.

_____

IMPROVING YOUR COMPOSITION SKILLS: DEVELOPING A STATEMENT WITH INCIDENTS

Helen Keller writes: "About this time I found out the use of a key."

Question: How does she develop this statement?
Answer: By narrating two incidents in which she uses a key to lock someone in.

In the first, the victim is her mother, and in the second, Miss Sullivan.

Exercise 16.11: Using an Incident

In a paragraph of about a hundred words, develop a statement with an incident. Here are some hints about how to begin:

Suggested Opening Sentences:

> A prank is not always funny.
> Every day we are reminded that smoke detectors save lives.
> People do not always appreciate the favors we do for them.
> Most accidents occur without warning.
> A kind word can change a person's outlook.
> Sometimes we learn the hard way.

Sample Paragraph Developed With an Incident

> **Every day we are reminded that smoke detectors save lives. Early one morning not too long ago, a distressed neighbor rushed into our house to ask us to call the fire department immediately. When the first engine arrived, the anxious firefighters at once demanded to know if all the people were out of the blazing house. We assured them that all our neighbors, including the dog, were safely accounted for. If the smoke detectors had not sounded, they might all have perished in that inferno.**

Now write your paragraph.

_____

_____

_____

_____

_____

_____

_____

_____

_____

_____

_____

_____

_____

_____

Review of Unit IV

Review IV.1: Vocabulary and Spelling

Fill in the missing letters of the *Word*. (Each space stands for one missing letter.) Then write the *Complete Word* in the blank space.

Definition	Word	Complete Word
1. proceed despite danger	VENT _ _ _	_____
2. noisy quarrel	SQ _ _ _ BLE	_____
3. playful or mischievous act	PR _ _ K	_____
4. person regarded with special liking	FAV _ _ _ TE	_____
5. in an unconvincing manner	LAM _ _ Y	_____
6. beyond what is usual	EXC _ _ _ IVE	_____
7. follow as a model	IMIT _ _ _	_____
8. greatest possible	_ _ MOST	_____
9. become less severe	REL _ _ T	_____
10. having a high-pitched sound	_ _ RILL	_____
11. freedom from punishment	IMPUN _ _ _	_____
12. merry game or party	_ _ OLIC	_____
13. cut in a straight line	SL _ _	_____
14. persuade by proof	_ _ _ VINCE	_____
15. indulge in idle talk	GOS _ _ _	_____
16. expression of regret for an offense	_ _ _ LOGY	_____
17. having a leaning or tendency	INCLI _ _ _	_____
18. hit hard repeatedly	POU _ _	_____
19. very unhappily	MIS _ _ _ BLY	_____
20. person entertained at the home of another	GU _ _ _	_____

Review IV.2: Synonyms

To each line, add a word that has the *same meaning* as the first two words on the line. Choose your words from the vocabulary list below.

1. suppose; guess _____

2. memory; remembrance _____

3. plain; unmistakable _____

4. furious; fierce _____

5. persistence; steadfastness _____

6. pull; twist _____

7. simple; nothing more than _____

8. influence; persuade _____

9. disquiet; anxiety _____

10. hurt; displease _____

Vocabulary List

distinct	violent
perseverance	induce
uneasiness	recollection
wrench	offend
conjecture	mere

Review IV.3: Antonyms

For each italicized word in column A, write the best *antonym* from column B.

	Column A	Column B
_____	1. *smiled* at me	occasionally
_____	2. *lenient* parents	combatted
_____	3. full of *glee*	dwindled
_____	4. slowly *increased*	relieved
_____	5. *championed* women's rights	foremost
_____	6. *strict* employer	gloom
_____	7. *customarily* late	indulgent
_____	8. *last* among the contestants	frowned
_____	9. *embarrassed* to hear my mark	obliging
_____	10. *inconsiderate* person	stern

Review IV.4: Spelling Challenges

Each word below is incomplete. Fill in the missing letter or letters.

In words 1–5, write S or SS.

1. occa_____ion
2. embarra_____ed
3. mi_____pelled
4. posse_____ion
5. unnece_____ary

In words 6–10, write IE or EI.

6. unbel_____vable
7. perc_____ve
8. conc_____vable
9. rel_____ve
10. rec_____ving

In words 11–15, add S or ES.

11. tomato_____
12. hero_____
13. radio_____
14. auto_____
15. potato_____

In words 16–20, add OR, ER, or AR.

16. elevat_____
17. li_____
18. offend_____
19. imitat_____
20. burgl_____

Review IV.5: Sentence Completion

Complete each sentence below with the most appropriate word from the following vocabulary list.

Vocabulary List

dwindled	inclined	imitated
shrill	combatted	distinct
ventured	indulgent	relented
conjectured	offended	embarrassed

1. When I apologized, my teacher quickly forgave me, but he said that next time he would be far less _____.

2. Father Marquette and Louis Joliet _____ down the Mississippi to the point where the Arkansas flows into it, and then they turned back.

3. I sometimes feel flustered when I have to make a speech in class. Do you, too, sometimes feel _____?

4. The hurt look in your eyes tells me that you were _____ by my remark.

5. At first the parents refused to let their children go on the trip, but after a while they _____ and gave their permission.

6. Both of the candidates believe in equality and have always _____ prejudice and injustice.

7. As the fog receded, the houses across the road became more _____.

8. Our treasury has _____ because we have had many expenses and some of the members have not yet paid their dues.

9. Physicians do not tend to become panicky in an emergency. They are _____ to remain calm.

10. A blue jay, protecting its nest, filled the air with _____ cries as a cat approached.

Review IV.6: Roots and Derivatives

On lines B and C, write the required forms of the italicized word on line A.

1. A. The joke did not *offend* anyone.

    B. The joke gave _____ to no one.

    C. The joke was not _____ to anyone.

2. A. Was there a note of *sternness* in her voice?

    B. Did she speak _____?

    C. Did she sound _____?

3. A. I do not *imitate* others.

    B. This is my own work, not an _____.

    C. I am not an _____.

4. A. Avoid *excessive* spending.

    B. Don't spend _____.

    C. See that your expenses do not _____ your income.

5. A. The witness could not *convince* me.

    B. The witness was not _____.

    C. The witness did not speak with _____.

6. A. Which is your *favorite* team?

    B. Which team do you _____?

    C. Which team is your _____?

7. A. The inhabitants live in *misery*.

    B. The inhabitants lead _____ lives.

    C. The inhabitants live _____.

8. A. They shouted *gleefully.*

    B. They gave a _____ shout.

    C. They shouted with _____.

9. A. She was ready to *apologize.*

    B. She was very _____.

    C. She quickly offered an _____.

10. A. The pupil lacked *perseverance.*

    B. The pupil was not _____.

    C. The pupil did not _____.

11. A. Many grandparents are *indulgent.*

    B. Many grandparents show _____.

    C. Many grandparents _____ their grandchildren.

12. A. Dave's father is very *obliging.*

    B. Dave's father _____ offered to drive us to the game.

    C. Dave's father is always ready to _____ us by giving us a lift.

13. A. I don't want to *embarrass* you.

    B. I don't want to put you into an _____ situation.

    C. I don't want to cause you any _____.

14. A. Do you feel *uneasy* about the future?

    B. Do you look to the future with _____?

    C. Do you regard the future _____?

15. A. There have been *occasions* when I was wrong.

    B. I have made an _____ error.

    C. _____ I have made a mistake.

16. A. Jay's *lameness* is gone.

    B. Jay is no longer _____.

    C. Jay no longer walks _____.

17. A. Can you see the letters *distinctly*?

    B. Can you _____ the letters?

    C. Are the letters _____?

18. A. The winds were *violent*.

    B. The winds blew _____.

    C. The winds blew with _____.

19. A. I did not recognize any of the *combatants*.

    B. I did not recognize any of the boys who took part in the _____.

    C. Tim did not participate in the fight because he is not _____.

20. A. We have not succeeded in *inducing* Mary to join the cheerleaders.

    B. Perhaps the new uniforms that we have been promised will _____ her to join.

    C. The new uniforms should be a powerful _____ to join our squad.

Review IV.7: Concise Writing

Rewrite the following fifty-three word paragraph, keeping all its ideas but reducing the number of words. Try to use no more than twenty-four words.

> Remember that a person who is being entertained in another person's home must not do anything to make anyone feel ill at ease. Therefore, do not indulge in idle talk or rumors about others, or quarrel noisily over trifles. The one who invited you is likely to look with disapproval on such behavior.

_____

_____

_____

_____

_____

_____

GENERAL INDEX

VOCABULARY INDEX